THERE IS NO EXAM

Your Commute to a Happier Life

ERIC SALINAS

Second Star Press

CONTENTS

Part Six
THE OPEN ROAD

Part Seven
TAKING THE WHEEL

Part Eight
PULLING OVER

To Silvana, my love & co-pilot, who sees the road the way I see it.
You showed me words could be vehicles.

PREFACE

Since I started living this way, my headaches diminished. Most of them were stress-related—tied to anxiety I didn't even realize I was carrying. I didn't cure stress. I just stopped adding fuel to a fire that was already burning.

The shift happened gradually. I started noticing patterns I couldn't unsee. Things everyone accepts as normal that maybe aren't as fixed as we think. Questions nobody asks because everyone assumes the answers are obvious.

Turns out, they're not.

I've been living differently for over a year now. It's not a method or routine—it's a mindset. Something fundamental changed in how I see goals, competition, success, what matters and what doesn't.

I started sharing this with a colleague at work. He told me it changed how he sees everything. That's one person. I figured if it resonated with him, maybe it would connect with someone else.

So, I decided to write this book.

Not to tell you how to live. Not to convert you to some philosophy. Just to share what I noticed, what shifted for me, and see if any of it connects with something you've sensed but couldn't name.

I'll share stories from my life. When something triggers your own memory, we're on track. When it doesn't, that's fine too. Different backgrounds mean different routes.

This is a conversation. I'm not here to package wisdom or perform expertise. I'm here to share what I learned by living it.

If you're reading this, you're already curious.

Ready? Let's start the engine.

INTRODUCTION: BUCKLE UP

Let's go for a ride (yes, in a car). I want to show you some things during this journey that you might recognize once you see them.

You know that feeling when you get into a brand-new car? The smell, the excitement of seeing everything for the first time. You start figuring out where the controls are. What this button does. Why that setting exists. As the days pass, you discover features you didn't even know were there. Some work exactly how you expected. Others surprise you completely.

That's how this book is going to feel. We'll be discovering things—pressing buttons we've never tried before, seeing what they actually do, learning that some things work completely differently than we thought. Things we took for granted might look different from this new angle.

We'll make stops along the way when we need to process what we're seeing. Stretch our legs. Sit with something for a moment before continuing.

You commute every day, right? To work, to school, to wherever you need to go. You know that drive. The familiar route. The traffic. The other cars around you.

This is your commute to a happier life.

You're not showing up empty-handed. You've lived long enough to have figured some things out. You've been through enough to have developed instincts. You've made enough choices to understand what matters to you. Whatever brought you to pick up this book—curiosity, frustration, timing, chance—you brought yourself here with everything you've already learned.

You know where your reference point is, and you may have passed several "obstacles" to get here. But now you are seeing some drivers on the road. And you are going to get to them, so that you can achieve the success you need. You've already realized who you are competing against. You already know what your 100% means. You know which choices brought you to this moment. You are here. You know not everyone will reach the same distance as you. Previous generations told you how to drive, but now you know your eyes just need to be focused on the road ahead. No distractions. You know all of this. You always have.

Ready? Take the wheel.

Part One

LEAVING YOUR NEIGHBORHOOD

Getting out of familiar territory, discovering new routes.

Chapter 1

YOU ARE HERE

There's something your brain does every single time you are in a car, and you've probably never realized it.

Ever notice how every driver faster than you is a reckless idiot, and every driver slower than you doesn't know what they're doing? That's not a coincidence. That's the setup for everything we're about to explore.

Driving in the Center Lane

We've left the neighborhood. Look at the car in the lane next to you. Now look at the one ahead. One of them is going faster than you, and now your brain immediately labels them: aggressive driver, probably rushing, thinks they own the road. The other one's going slower, and your brain does it again: why are they even in this lane? Didn't they teach them to grab the right lane if they drive slowly?

Here's the thing: both reactions happened because of YOUR speed. You are the reference point. You are the zero on the speedometer of your world.

That car going 80 mph? They're looking at someone going 90 mph thinking the exact same thing you just thought about them. And the car you just called slow? They're looking at someone going even slower with the same frustration you felt about them.

Everyone is the center of their own references. You may have heard that you're not the center of the universe but you are absolutely the center of YOUR universe, of YOUR life. Everything you perceive as "fast" or "slow," "smart" or "stupid," "successful" or "struggling" is being measured against you as the baseline.

The Infinite Competition Loop

And this creates a problem. Once you measure yourself against everyone else, you get trapped in an infinite loop.

Let's say you're cruising along and you see someone ahead going faster. You speed up to pass them. Feels good, right? But wait—now you can see a new car ahead going even faster than you. So you speed up again. Pass them too.

Except now there's another car you couldn't see before, going even faster than that one.

And another one beyond that.

And another one beyond that. And another.

You didn't actually get anywhere different in the competition. You just changed which cars you're comparing yourself to. The moment you pass the "faster" cars, you simply reveal a NEW set of faster cars you couldn't see before. You think we need one more? There's always one more car ahead. It never ends.

This isn't just about highway driving. This is about everything.

Salaries: "I make $80k" feels good until you meet someone making $120k, then someone making $200k, then someone making $2M...

Fitness: "I can bench press 150 lbs" until you see someone doing 200, then 250, then 400...

Followers: "I have 1,000 followers" until you see someone with 10k, then 100k, then 1M, you don't have a YouTube plate? pfft...

The loop never closes because you keep moving the comparison point every time you think you've "arrived."

Your Odometer, Not Their Speed

So here's the shift: stop looking at other cars' speeds. Look at your own odometer. Your miles traveled.

Your odometer measures distance traveled, not speed. Yesterday your odometer read 1,000 miles. Today it reads 1,050. That's progress. Fifty more miles of experience, learning, living. That's the only measurement that matters.

Some days you'll travel 100 miles because the highway is wide open, and the weather is perfect. Some days you'll travel 10 miles because you're on a mountain road that requires careful navigation. Both days added miles to your odometer. Both days moved you forward.

Maybe today you're driving at 50 mph and yesterday you were cruising at 65 mph. That doesn't mean you're regressing. It might mean today's road requires you to slow down and admire the landscape—driving down the coastline with the ocean beside you—or navigate carefully through difficult terrain. The speed doesn't matter. The miles you're accumulating do.

The person next to you going faster or slower? Their odometer is reading completely different numbers because they started from a different place, took different routes, made different stops. Their mileage has nothing to do with your journey. Have a safe journey.

Compare your odometer to YOUR odometer from yesterday. That's the only comparison that means anything.

The Lane Ownership Illusion

And while we're challenging false competition, let's address another illusion you've been carrying: ownership of public space.

You're driving as usual, coming back from work. You just want to make it in time to your partner, who's waiting for you at home to go to the movies. You were momentarily distracted and suddenly didn't notice a car cut in front of you—you slammed on the brakes, but ended up rear-ending them.

Minor accident. No one got hurt. The plans? Gone. The movie will have to wait. Everybody makes sure the other driver is okay. Car insurances arrive. Traffic cop too. You tell your story to the officer. "I was driving below the speed limit and suddenly this car merged into my lane. I just couldn't brake on time..."

Right there. Let's zoom out. The real story isn't about the accident —this hypothetical was just to point out something. "Your lane"?

When did that lane become yours? Did you buy it? Is your name on the title? Do you get deed papers when you merge onto the highway?

The lanes are public. They belong to everyone. That other driver has just as much right to that lane as you do.

But what happens when you think you own the lane: road rage. The moment you believe that space is YOURS, any car entering it feels like a violation. Like someone breaking into your house. Your stress levels spike because someone "took" something from you.

Except they didn't. Because it was never yours to begin with.

I'm not saying you have to love it when someone merges without signaling or cuts you off. I'm saying the intensity of your anger is directly proportional to how much ownership you feel over public space.

Lowering the Road Rage

Look, I will not tell you never to honk or never to get frustrated. That's not realistic, and honestly, it's not even the goal (and I would be a terrible living example if I said otherwise).

Sometimes you SHOULD honk. If someone's about to hit you, honk. If someone doesn't realize the light turned green and traffic is backing up, a quick honk is helpful. If someone's drifting into your lane, honk for safety.

The goal isn't zero road rage. The goal is maybe 10% road rage instead of 90%.

Be human. Get annoyed sometimes. But be intentional about it. Ask yourself: "Is this honk for safety, or is it for my ego?". Also consider others and occasionally honk for them, for their security. Sometimes they need it.

If a car cuts you off and you lean on the horn for 10 seconds while yelling, that's ego. You're not preventing an accident at that point—the car already cut you off. You're just punishing them for disrespecting "your" lane. Revenge is a funny thing. And there's always someone watching.

Your honking won't change their behavior. They'll either not care, or they'll get defensive, or they'll flip you off. Nobody has ever had a road rage moment and thought, "You know what, that angry honking really taught me a valuable lesson about changing lanes."

The Only Coordinate That Matters

So let's establish the foundational rule for this entire journey:

You are your own [0,0] in your [x, y] coordinate.

Everything around you—speed, success, intelligence, beauty, wealth —is being measured relative to YOUR position. And that's not arrogance. That's just physics. You can't measure anything without a reference point, and you are YOUR reference point.

Other people are THEIR reference points. They're measuring you relative to them, just like you're measuring them relative to you.

Nobody's wrong. Everyone's just driving their own route at their own pace with their own odometer showing different numbers.

The problem isn't that you're the center of your own universe. The problem is thinking you're supposed to be the center of EVERY-ONE'S universe. Or worse, believing there's some objective scorecard in the sky grading everyone's driving performance.

There isn't.

There is no exam.

So, stop comparing your speed to others. Stop thinking you own the lane. Stop honking at every perceived slight. Focus on YOUR route, YOUR progress, YOUR odometer compared to where it was yesterday.

That's where we're starting. Right here. At YOUR coordinates.

Ready to keep going?

Chapter 2

10,000 REARVIEW MIRRORS

Unlike anything else in your life, your car reveals different versions of who you are.

Remember all the times you've had passengers. Kids in the backseat on the way to school. A spouse riding shotgun during a road trip. Elderly parents on the way to a doctor's appointment. Friends piling in for a weekend getaway. A coworker you gave a ride to when their car was in the shop.

Each of them experienced a completely different driver. A different world from the passenger seat.

Not because you were being fake. Not because you were putting on a show. But different situations, different passengers, and different roads bring out different versions of who you are behind the wheel.

Different Passengers, Different Drivers

If you have kids, think about those family road trips. You're gripping the steering wheel too tight, worrying out loud about gas money. You're snapping at them to "stop fighting back there" because traffic is stressing you out.

There's tension in your voice when you get lost and refuse to trust the GPS. You think they're focused on the destination—the beach, the theme park, the mountains. But they're not.

They're focused on you. Kids absorb everything. They're watching the driver. Because the driver controls their safety, their comfort, their entire experience in that car.

They're not thinking about where they're going. They're watching how you're getting them there.

Now think about your spouse or partner riding shotgun.

They see a completely different driver than your kids do. They see you making quick route changes when you're running late—switching lanes aggressively, taking shortcuts, pushing yellow lights. But they also see you in the parking lot, taking extra time to back into a spot perfectly because you don't want to leave the car crooked.

They see impatient you and meticulous you on the same trip.

Your kids only see "stressed driver." Your spouse sees the nuance— the competence mixed with impatience, the care mixed with frustration. They know you're not just one driver; you're several drivers depending on the context.

When your elderly parents are in the car? Suddenly, you're a different driver entirely.

You slow down at yellow lights instead of speeding through them. You leave extra space between you and the car ahead. You avoid lane changes unless absolutely necessary. You narrate your driving decisions out loud: "I'm going to merge now, just letting that car pass first."

This isn't fake. This is appropriate. This is you adapting your driving to your passengers' needs.

But if your kids could see THIS version of you, they'd barely recognize the driver. Where's the person who yells at slow drivers and cuts through side streets to save three minutes?

And then there are those weekend trips with friends—windows down, music up, taking the scenic route because nobody's in a hurry. You're driving 10 mph under the speed limit just to enjoy the view. You're stopping at random roadside diners. You're laughing at wrong turns instead of stressing about them.

Your spouse would be shocked. "Since when do you enjoy getting lost?"

But you're not a different person. You're just a different driver in a different context with different passengers and different stakes.

Every weekday at 2 p.m., you're in the school pickup line. Patient. Safety-focused. Slowly inching forward. Waving other parents ahead of you. Making sure no kids run behind your car.

But three hours later, you're leaving work in rush hour traffic. It's on. Aggressively changing lanes because you need to get home, make dinner, and get the kids to soccer practice by 6.

Same driver. Same day. Completely different approaches.

So which one is the "real" you?

All of them.

Every single version is authentic. You're not putting on a mask—you're responding to different roads, different passengers, different circumstances.

If you tried to drive in a way that would satisfy ALL your past passengers at the same time, you'd be paralyzed. It's insane to even try.

Your kids would want you calm and relaxed. Your spouse would want you decisive and efficient. Your elderly parents would want you cautious and slow. Your friends would want you spontaneous and fun.

You'd need to be 10,000 different drivers to impress everyone who's ever been in your car.

The Impossible Perfect Version

We create this idealized version in our heads—the "perfect driver" that would make everyone happy. Calm but decisive. Patient but efficient. Careful but spontaneous.

And then we exhaust ourselves trying to BE that version for everyone, all the time.

We think everyone is grading us on how close we get to this perfect version. We imagine our passengers comparing notes: "When I rode with them, they were really stressed. What happened to the fun, relaxed version they're supposed to be?"

That universal perfect version doesn't exist. It never did.

You're not failing to become it. You're chasing something that was never possible in the first place.

Your kids don't need the fun road-trip version when they're scared in the backseat during a storm—they need the confident, I've-got-this version. Your elderly parents don't need the efficient version—they need the patient, careful version. Your spouse doesn't need the always-happy version—they need the honest, authentic version.

There is no exam grading whether you've become the "right" version of yourself. There's just different roads requiring different approaches, and different passengers needing different things from you.

Stop trying to perfect one universal you. Start recognizing which version genuinely serves the moment you're in.

Choosing Your Passengers

You can't be all versions at once. But you can choose which version serves you best for the route you're on right now.

If you're taking your kids somewhere, maybe channel the patient, narrating-every-decision version instead of the stressed, hurried version. Not because one is "real" and the other is fake, but because one creates better memories for the passengers who matter most on that particular trip.

If you're driving alone to clear your head, maybe channel the scenic route version instead of the aggressive efficiency version. Not because you're "supposed to" relax, but because that version might actually serve your needs better in that moment.

Some people bring out driving behaviors in you that you don't particularly like.

Maybe there's a passenger who makes you feel judged, so you drive more cautiously than you need to—second-guessing every lane change, over-explaining every decision. Or maybe there's a passenger who makes you feel competitive, so you drive more aggressively to prove something.

The question isn't "Which version is the real me?" The question is, "Which version do I want to be, and who do I want riding with me?"

You choose who gets in your car. You choose who rides shotgun. You choose who influences your driving.

Some passengers make you a better driver. Some passengers stress you out. Some passengers you enjoy having around. Some passengers you're only giving a ride to out of obligation.

There is no exam grading which passengers you should keep or which version of yourself you should be. But there is a choice about who gets access to your car and which routes you take with them.

Let Them Keep Their Version

Something that might make you uncomfortable: the people in your life have already formed their version of you. And you have no idea of how that version is. It's like when you hear yourself on a recording. It might not match the version you think you are—or the version you're trying to show them.

Let's say your kid tells a story at Thanksgiving: "Remember that road trip where Dad got so lost and we ended up at that weird diner? That was hilarious!"

But you remember it differently. You weren't lost—you took a deliberate detour. And you were stressed out of your mind, not having fun.

You have two choices:

Option A: Correct them. "Actually, I wasn't lost. I was taking a scenic route, and I was pretty stressed about it, not laughing."

Option B: Let them keep their version. Because in THEIR memory, that moment is a happy one. They remember laughing with their siblings. They remember the quirky diner. They remember you as part of an adventure, not a mistake.

Why would you take that away from them just to be technically correct?

Their version fulfills them, not your corrected version. Their "twisted" memory of you is what they love. It's what they need from that moment. Your corrected version doesn't serve them—it serves your ego's need to be understood accurately.

This applies to everyone. Your spouse remembers the version of you that matters to them in their story—often a version you're not even conscious of, a version you haven't realized you are. The amazing one they married. The one who makes them feel safe, or seen, or challenged in just the right way. Your parents remember the version that fits their experience. Your friends remember the version from the time in their lives when you were present.

You can't make them update their version to match your current reality. And honestly, why would you want to?

Let people keep their version of you. As long as it's not harmful, as long as it brings them something they need, let them have it.

You're not one fixed driver captured perfectly in everyone's memory. You're 10,000 versions in 10,000 distinct memories, and every single one of those versions is real. They are here to stay in those memories, whether you like it or not.

There's no exam requiring you to correct everyone's memory to match your official story.

You're Not Trapped

You're not one fixed driver. You're a collection of driving styles that show up in different contexts.

But just because you CAN drive stressed, impatient, and worried doesn't mean you HAVE TO keep driving that way—especially if it's not beneficial for you or the passengers you actually care about.

You can't control how your past passengers remember you. Your kids might remember the stressed version even though you tried your best. That's not under your control.

But you can control how you drive from here forward. You can decide which version shows up more often. You can decide which passengers get regular access to your car.

You're not trapped being the driver everyone else experienced. You get to choose which version takes the wheel tomorrow.

There's no exam at the end grading whether you chose "correctly." There's just you, your car, your route, and the passengers you decide to bring along.

So who do you want to be behind that wheel?

Part Two

HIGHWAY ENTRANCE

Getting on the highway, realizing how you learned to drive.

Chapter 3

THE ROUTES THEY TAUGHT YOU

R emember when you first learned everything you know about driving? Not just the mechanics—how to turn the wheel, press the pedals, check your mirrors. I'm talking about the other stuff. The unwritten rules. The instincts. The gut reactions you have when someone cuts you off or when you see an open parking spot.

Where did those come from?

How Knowledge Spreads

Let's say, a pencil.

You know you can write with it, but how do you know it? Your teacher told you, maybe your parents. But that specific knowledge went "viral" thousands of years ago. And before your teacher, someone taught them. And before that, someone else. Going back hundreds, maybe thousands of years—the pencil "knowledge virus" is still alive, still spreading, still transmitting the same basic idea: this tool makes marks on paper.

I mean, we now literally know what going viral means.

(I know that some may have blocked out 2020, but we experienced firsthand how something literally went viral.)

If you had COVID, imagine how many people before you carried the same virus strain as yours. If you go back, there's one origin, patient zero, then it went "viral" from several people up to you. Technically, that virus went through many, many people, like you were the 73rd generation.

Knowledge works the same way. It spreads from person to person, generation to generation, each one passing it along, and most of the time, without questioning where it originally came from.

That's how we basically learn everything.

The Driving Habits You Inherited

You learned to drive at a driving school—where they taught you the official rules (and maybe some instructors' personal pet peeves). From your parents, who taught you by example every time you sat in the backseat watching them. From your culture, which taught you that certain driving behaviors mean certain things. From the movies, which showed you what "cool" driving looks like, what "aggressive" driving looks like, what "success" looks like on the road.

None of this is neutral. All of it is programming.

Competitive lane-changing? You learned that. Maybe from watching your mom or dad weave through traffic to "make up time." Maybe from movies where the hero always drives like a rocket. Maybe from your city's driving culture, where hesitation gets you honked at.

Status parking spots? You learned that too. Getting there first. Parking close to the entrance. Having the "best" spot. None of that is objectively better—it's just a hierarchy someone made up and everyone agreed to enforce.

Road hierarchy? Trucks should stay right. Sports cars get to go fast. Minivans are boring. Luxury cars deserve respect. EVs are for environmentalists (or early adopters, depending on which virus you caught).

All learned. All transmitted. All accepted without question.

Someone Told You to Feel Superior

Neil deGrasse Tyson—astrophysicist, science communicator, someone I deeply admire for how he embraces ideas—wrote something about competition in his book *Starry Messenger* that applies perfectly here:

> The Olympics owes its existence to the search for people who perform faster, higher, and stronger among us. Standardized exams, game shows, beauty contests, talent auditions, and the Forbes 400 all pit humans against humans, in rank order. Society offers hundreds, if not thousands of ways to show you're better than others.[1]

And then he said something that should make us all stop and think:

> "You feel superior because somebody told you it was ok to feel that way."[2]

Let that sink in.

You didn't wake up one day naturally feeling like you're better than the slow driver clogging up the left lane when they should be in the right lane. Someone taught you that slow drivers in the left lane are "wrong" even though they are driving at the speed limit, and therefore you (the faster, "correct" driver) are superior.

You didn't inherently know that passing more cars means winning. Someone taught you that getting ahead = success.

The competition was installed in you. Like software. Like a virus.

My Hometown's Attention Economy

Let me give you a personal example from where I was born.

I grew up in Monterrey, Mexico, and there's a deeply embedded cultural virus there. We call ourselves competitors and hard workers, and we brag about that with pride—but maybe we're just masking the need for attention and validation to feel superior to others.

Here's how it works: If someone has something that receives attention, you need something better, bigger, (usually more expensive) to get —or steal—the spotlight from them.

Your friend buys a car that people notice? You will look for a truck that people notice more.

Your neighbor throws a party everyone's talking about? You need to throw one that becomes the new standard.

It applies to everything. Weddings. *Quinceañeras*. Job titles. House sizes. Sports teams.

And here's the twisted part: your joy becomes relative to making others feel less.

It's not enough to be happy with your car—you need to know your car gets more attention than your friend's car. It's not enough to throw a wonderful party—you need people to say it was better than the last one, so the previous host feels outdone.

And it's not only with events and possessions. It gets even more personal:

"When are you getting married?" "When are you having kids?" "Your cousin already has two kids, what are you waiting for?" "Your brother just got promoted, how's your job going?"

This constant comparison doesn't come from some objective measurement system. It's the same cultural virus spreading through families, convincing everyone that their worth is measured by hitting the same milestones—and hitting them more impressively than everyone else.

There's even a thought experiment that exposes this perfectly:

"Would you rather have a $300,000 house where everyone else has $200,000 houses, or a $500,000 house where everyone else has $1,000,000 houses?"

Rationally, the half-million dollar house is objectively better. Bigger, nicer, more valuable.

But most people pick the $300,000 house. Because in that neighborhood, they're winning. They're at the top. Abundance doesn't matter if you're not relatively superior. They have the nicest house on the block—they're getting all the attention.

In the million-dollar neighborhood, they're at the bottom. They have the "worst" house. Even though it's still a mansion by any objective measure, nobody's paying attention to them.

That preference—to be relatively superior rather than objectively better—is learned. It's a cultural virus. And it makes people miserable.

This isn't everyone, and it's not just Monterrey. But it's what I know from growing up there.

Status Signals We're Taught to Care About

Ever notice how some people only buy expensive coffee from the trending place when they could make coffee at home for a fraction of the price (but without the cup)?

It's not about the coffee. It's about walking into the office with that specific cup. It's about being seen as someone who can afford the "nice" coffee from the place everyone's talking about. It's status signaling.

Same with brand clothes where the logo is enormous and visible. You're not buying the quality (a plain shirt is just as functional)—you're buying the signal. You're saying, "I can afford this brand, which means I'm above people who can't."

And you can always tell when someone just got rich overnight because suddenly they're wearing big logos and brand patterns all over their outfit. They need to show the crowd that they can afford it. They seem like walking luxury brand totems.

Nobody is born caring about logos. That's learned. That's a virus someone spread, and you caught it.

Back in my high school years, one time I was hanging out with a couple of friends back in my hometown. We were just calling it a night after being on the skateboard all day (there was no internet back then, so we socialized outdoors—crazy times, huh?). We were sitting in the garage of my friend's house, and there was a car parked at the neighbor's.

I don't remember the exact details, but the conversation led to us noticing it just as a standard-shaped car. Gray. Boring. We were like, "Meh, it's a sedan."

But then one friend walked by to throw his cigarette and realized it was a BMW, and suddenly he started saying, "Wow, look at it, that's an amazing car!"

The brand made him think that way. Not the car itself. Not anything objectively different from its appearance or function. Just the logo. Just the knowledge that it was "supposed to be" impressive.

That's the virus in action. We didn't care about the car until we knew it was expensive. Then we cared because we were supposed to care.

When You Catch Yourself Caring

Cultural programming is effective because it runs silently. You don't notice it installing. You just feel the reaction and assume it's yours.

But you can learn to spot it in the moment.

You're at a stoplight and a luxury car pulls up next to you. Something happens in your brain—an automatic judgment about the driver, maybe a flash of envy or a sense of superiority depending on what you're driving. That reaction wasn't yours. It was programmed into you.

You see someone's vacation photos on social media. Before you even think about it, you're comparing their trip to yours, especially if you've already been there a while ago, feeling like you're behind, mentally planning the next even more impressive vacation to post about. That comparison reflex wasn't yours. It was installed.

The programming shows up in the split second between seeing something and feeling something about it. That gap—that's where the installed beliefs live.

You can't erase cultural programming completely. It's too deep. Too automatic. Too reinforced by everything around you.

But you can learn to recognize it. And recognition changes everything.

When you catch yourself judging someone's car, house, clothes, job—you can pause and ask: "Where did I learn that this matters?" Start looking up the origin of your own beliefs.

When you feel the urge to one-up someone's story, you can notice:

"Do I actually want to share this, or am I just trying to establish hierarchy?"

When you start comparing your life to someone else's highlight reel, you can catch yourself: "Who taught me to measure my worth this way?"

You won't always choose differently. Sometimes you'll recognize the programming and still follow its instructions because it's easier, or because everyone else is following it too, or because you're too tired to resist.

But recognition breaks the autopilot. It creates a moment of choice where there used to be just automatic reaction. And that moment—that's where freedom starts.

You Can Unlearn

Here's the good news: if these ideas were learned, they can be unlearned.

You're not stuck with the driving habits you inherited. You're not required to compete just because everyone around you is competing. You're not obligated to feel superior just because your culture told you it's okay.

You can recognize the programming for what it is—an idea that was transmitted to you without your permission—and decide whether you want to keep it.

Some cultural programming is useful. Traffic laws exist for good reasons. Social norms around basic courtesy make society function.

But competitive lane-changing? Status parking? Feeling superior because you drive a certain way or because you have a sunroof?

Those are optional. And they're making you miserable.

So how do you actually start unlearning?

Start with awareness. You just practiced that in the last section. Notice when the programming is running. Don't judge it. Don't fight it immediately. Just see it. "Oh, there's that automatic status comparison again."

Then question it. When you catch the programming running, ask yourself: "What if I didn't care about this?" Not as a commitment to stop caring forever—just as an experiment. What if that person's car didn't matter? What if you didn't need the impressive vacation? What if you just... let it be? The world doesn't end. Usually, nothing happens at all.

Then try choosing differently once. Not as a new rule. Not as a permanent change. Just once. Someone's talking about something they're proud of. Instead of mentioning your own achievement, just say, "That's great." That's it. Not "You just made my day", not making it about yourself. Just plain recognition. See what happens. Usually? They keep talking. They don't notice you didn't compete. The hierarchy you thought you needed to establish wasn't actually necessary.

Notice how it feels. When you don't take part in a comparison you normally would've engaged in, when you don't buy the status item you usually would've bought, when you don't judge someone you normally would've judged—pay attention to the feeling. Sometimes it's a relief. Sometimes it's freedom. Sometimes it's uncomfortable because the programming is still there, still insisting this matters. All of those feelings are information.

That's unlearning. Not erasing the code. Not replacing it with different code. Just recognizing it's code, and deciding whether you want to run it.

You can choose to stop taking part in competitions you never agreed to enter. You can choose to stop measuring your happiness against other people's lives. You can choose to drive your own route without worrying about whether you're "ahead" or "behind" anyone else.

There is no exam grading whether you're keeping up with the right people or following the right cultural script.

But there is a choice: keep running the software someone else installed, or start writing your own code.

Chapter 4

THE SPEED TRAP

Knowing what others think about us used to require actual feedback. Now we get instant metrics: likes, views, shares. And we've become addicted to the scoreboard of a race we didn't agree to run.

Why are we racing? Who told us we needed to be the fastest car on the highway? When did documenting our lives become more important than living them?

The Concert Evolution

There's a perfect example of how this shift happened, and you can trace it through concerts over the last 40 years:

- 1980s: People went to concerts with their hands up, lighters flickering in the dark. They were experiencing the music. They were IN the moment. The goal was to feel the music, to be part of the crowd energy, to connect with the performance.
- 1990s: Cameras came out. People started taking pictures of the band members. Most of the times it was forbidden to

introduce cameras to a concert. But when you can, the pictures were to remember them the night later. To look back and say, "I saw them live." The experience was still primary. The documentation was secondary.

- 2000s: Cell phones got cameras. Now people were recording entire songs—pixelated, terrible audio, shaky footage that they'd never actually watch again. But they were still mostly watching the show while they recorded. The phone was supplementary to the experience.
- 2010s: Smartphones got better. Now people were taking selfies WITH the band in the background. Notice the shift? The band became the backdrop. The concert wasn't about the performance anymore—it was about proving YOU were at the performance. The documentation was becoming equivalent to the experience.
- 2020s: Now? Now, people film themselves throughout the entire concert. The camera facing them, the band fades out in the horizon behind their phone. The performers don't matter—we are the protagonists of our own event called "attending a concert." They're not watching the show. They're watching their screen capturing themselves at the show.

We've become the story. The band is irrelevant.

The concert isn't the destination anymore. The concert is just the backdrop for your content. For your story. For your proof that you're living an interesting life that other people should be impressed by.

Everyone's Performing, Nobody's Watching

There's a video that went viral a few years ago. The saddest thing is that is repeating itself each year. New Year's Eve in Paris. Thousands of people gathered around the *Arc de Triomphe* for the midnight celebration.

The camera pans across the crowd. Every single person has their phone up, recording. Everyone.

Not watching. Recording.

Nobody is experiencing the moment they traveled thousands of miles to see. They're all watching it through a 6-inch screen, making sure they capture it for people who aren't there.

So, if everyone's recording and nobody's watching, what's the point of being there?

Who are they recording it for? The people who weren't there? Why would those people care about shaky phone footage of something they didn't experience?

The answer: they're recording it to prove they were there. To prove their life is interesting. To collect evidence that they're winning the race.

Go to any gym now. Watch what happens.

Someone sets up their phone to record their workout. Not to check their form. Not to track their progress. To post it. To show everyone that they're working out. That they're committed. That they're better than the people who aren't at the gym.

And here's where it gets really revealing: they'll kick people out of their camera shot. They'll get annoyed if someone walks through their frame. They'll restart their set because someone "ruined" their video.

And then—this is where it gets even worse—they'll post the video exposing the person who dared to interrupt their recording. How dare they use the public gym while someone is filming content? They'll shame strangers online for the crime of... existing in a shared space. (Shout out to Joey Swoll—a bodybuilder and fitness influencer—for starting the "Mind Your Own Business" movement to call out this behavior.)

The workout becomes secondary to the documentation of the workout.

They're not there to get stronger. They're there to be seen getting stronger. They're not competing against their previous performance—they're competing for attention, for validation, for proof that they're ahead in the race.

Where's the Reality Show?

Social media changed the dynamics of how we see ourselves. It taught us that we're all the main character in our own movie, and everyone else should be watching.

We're not just living our lives. We're performing our life. We're curating our lives. We're editing our lives for an audience that may or may not actually care.

We act like we're playing a game we never signed up for—reality show contestants, constantly aware of the camera, constantly adjusting our behavior for the viewers, constantly measuring our worth by the ratings.

But the uncomfortable truth: nobody is watching as closely as you think they are.

Your followers aren't studying your posts. They're scrolling. They're half-paying attention while they wait in line for coffee. They're consuming your content the same way you're consuming theirs—quickly, mindlessly, already forgetting it before they move to the next post.

Psychologists call this the spotlight effect. You assume you're on stage, that everyone notices your appearance, your mistakes, your life choices. The truth? Everyone is too worried about themselves to worry about you. They're not the audience watching your movie—they're the stars of their own movie, barely aware you exist as anything other than background scenery.

You're racing for attention from people who aren't actually watching the race.

Swipe Down to Refresh

So why can't we stop? Why do we keep checking? Why does it feel so hard to just put the phone down?

Because the system is designed to hook you.

Social media platforms aren't just apps—they're slot machines in your pocket. And they use the exact same psychological mechanism that makes gambling addictive: intermittent reinforcement.

Here's how it works: You post something. You don't know how it will perform. Maybe it gets 10 likes. Maybe 100. Maybe 1,000. That uncertainty creates anticipation. And anticipation triggers dopamine.

Every time you check your phone, you're pulling the lever on a slot machine. Sometimes you win (notifications! likes! comments!). Sometimes you don't. But the possibility that THIS time might be the big win keeps you checking.

The dopamine hit isn't even from the likes themselves—it's from the anticipation of maybe getting likes. That's why you keep refreshing. That's why you check five minutes after posting. That's why you feel anxious when a post isn't performing as well as you expected.

You're not weak. You're not addicted because you lack willpower. You're up against a multi-billion dollar industry that has engineered these platforms specifically to be as addictive as possible. They employ neuroscientists and behavioral psychologists whose entire job is to figure out how to keep you scrolling.

The red notification badge? Designed to trigger urgency. The infinite scroll? Designed to eliminate stopping points. The "seen" indicator? Designed to create social pressure to respond immediately. The algorithm showing you content that gets you riled up? Designed to keep you engaged even if it makes you miserable.

Every feature is optimized for one thing: keeping you on the platform as long as possible so they can sell more ads. The algorithm is governing what you see, what you feel, what you do next.

And it works because dopamine doesn't care about your wellbeing. Dopamine cares about reward prediction. Your mind doesn't distinguish between real or imagined rewards—dopamine fires either way. And these platforms have figured out exactly how to hack that system.

That's why you can spend two hours scrolling and feel worse than when you started. That's why you can know intellectually that social media is making you anxious but still can't stop checking. That's why deleting the app feels like withdrawal.

You're not failing at self-control. You're fighting a system specifically designed to override your self-control.

Chasing Validation from Ghosts

So why do we do it? Why do we keep feeding the machine even when we know it's designed to exploit us?

Because in our mind, we're looking for validation that we're cooler than others. That we're more interesting. That we're winning the race.

Every post is a comparison. Every story is evidence. Every like is a vote confirming that yes, you're ahead, you're doing better, you're worth paying attention to.

The concert isn't about the music—it's about proving you have access to concerts other people don't. The gym video isn't about fitness —it's about proving you're more disciplined than people who aren't at the gym. The vacation photos aren't about the vacation—they're about proving your life is more exciting than the people scrolling past your posts.

Social media turned life into a performance review. And we've been chasing a good grade ever since.

There's no judge. There's no final score. There's no panel of people at the end of your life reviewing your Instagram feed and deciding if you lived correctly.

You're racing in a competition that doesn't exist, trying to impress people who aren't paying attention, collecting points that mean nothing.

Documentation vs Performance

When you stop performing, you get to actually live. You get to be present. You get to experience moments instead of just capturing evidence that they happened. You get your attention back. You get your life back.

People are waking up to this. They're realizing they've spent years filming their lives instead of living them. And they're making a change: share less, experience more.

But let me be clear: documenting moments isn't the problem. Taking photos to remember your kid's first concert? Beautiful. Recording a video message for someone who couldn't be there?

Thoughtful. Capturing a moment because you genuinely want to revisit it later? Perfectly fine.

The problem is when documentation becomes performance.

So ask yourself:

Were you sharing because you wanted to remember the moment? Or were you sharing because you wanted others to see you having the moment?

Were you documenting your life? Or were you performing your life?

Were you experiencing the concert? Or were you proving you were at the concert?

There's nothing wrong with the first option in each question. Memory matters. Connection matters. Sharing meaningful moments with people you care about—that's human.

But when every moment becomes content, when every experience becomes evidence in a competition you didn't agree to enter, when your life is curated for an audience instead of lived for yourself—that's when you've lost the road.

There is no exam grading whether your life looks impressive to strangers on the internet.

But there is a choice: keep racing for validation from people who aren't watching, or put the phone down and actually experience what you're doing.

The highway is long. The scenery is worth seeing. But you can't see it if you're staring at a screen showing you what other people think of you.

Stop competing for attention. Stop racing to prove you're ahead. Stop filming the drive and just... drive.

Chapter 5

WHO'S KEEPING SCORE?

Imagine risking everything you've worked for over an argument with a stranger.

And I mean everything.

The education—all those years attending school, playing at recess, growing up praising your sports idol, learning your favorite singer's lyrics. Going out with your friends. Spending time with your folks when they took you on vacations. All the hard work they put in to get you into college. The shifts you worked to pay for your education. The uncountable nights you didn't sleep, studying for those brutal classes, pushing through because you were building toward something.

The home you've built with your partner. The people waiting for you at home. Your brothers or siblings who've known you your whole life. Your children, who don't ever think that something might happen to their hero. They depend on you completely—for their education, for their shelter, for their safety, for their future.

All of it. Everything you've built. Everything you've sacrificed for. Everything you've worked toward. Everything you'll leave something behind for.

Over an argument with a stranger about a game. Or a lane change. Or who was right. Over someone who isn't my people.

Sounds crazy, right?

People do it every day.

The Stadium Fight

You're at a game. Your team scores. You celebrate. The guy sitting behind you—wearing the other team's jersey—says something. Not even to you, just muttering to his friend. But you heard it.

Now you have a choice.

You could ignore it. Enjoy the game. Go home to your family. Wake up tomorrow with your job intact, your health intact, your life intact.

Or you could turn around and say something back. Escalate. Let it become a thing. Let your ego convince you that you need to put this stranger in his place because he disrespected your team, which means he disrespected you, which means you have to defend your honor.

And then what happens?

Maybe nothing. Maybe he'll back down. Maybe you both yell and then security separates you and you both go home feeling like you "won."

Or maybe it turns physical. Maybe you throw a punch. Maybe he throws one back. Maybe you fall. Maybe you hit your head on a concrete step. Maybe you lose an eye. Maybe you end up paralyzed. Maybe you end up in jail.

For what?

For your team? I mean, they usually don't know you exist as an individual. They're not going to visit you at the hospital. They're not going to pay your legal fees. They're not going to take care of your kids while you're dealing with a brain injury.

For your pride? How much is your pride worth? Is it worth your ability to walk? Is it worth your children losing a good dad or mom over a stranger's insult? Is it worth your children watching their parent get arrested? Is it worth losing your job because you have a criminal record now?

Well, the thing is, there is no judge awarding points for being right.

You don't get a grade at the end of the confrontation. There's no panel reviewing the footage and declaring, "Yes, you were correct to escalate this situation. Here's your trophy for defending your honor." Fanfares. Fireworks. You did it!

You just get the consequences. And the other guy gets his consequences. And both of you risked everything for... nothing.

The Traffic Confrontation

Same pattern, different location.

Someone cuts you off in traffic. Maybe they didn't see you. Maybe they're rushing to the hospital. Maybe they're just an inconsiderate driver. Doesn't matter—you're angry.

You have the same choice as the stadium guy. Victim or not, make a decision.

Ignore it and keep driving. Or make it a thing.

You speed up. You pull alongside them. You yell. You gesture. You lay on your horn. You follow them. You want them to know they were wrong. You want them to feel bad. You want to win this confrontation.

The really stupid part? Being "right" won't stop their car from hitting you.

Let's say they cut you off badly. Let's say you're 100% in the right, and they're 100% in the wrong, and if this went to traffic court, the judge would side with you completely.

Congratulations. You're right.

But if their car hits yours because you decided to prove a point by not letting them merge, being right doesn't matter. Your car gets damaged. You might get injured. You might end up in a hospital.

The laws of physics don't care about traffic laws. The other driver's insurance doesn't care that you were technically correct. Your funeral doesn't get a banner that says, "BUT HE HAD THE RIGHT OF WAY."

There is no exam grading whether you were justified or not in your road rage.

There's just the outcome. And the outcome might be that you're right AND you're hurt. Or you're right, AND you're in a hospital. Or you're right, AND you're dealing with a lawsuit for causing an accident.

Take care of yourself. No one else is watching out for you on the road.

The Invisible Scorekeepers

So who do you think is grading you?

When you feel that pull to defend your honor, to prove someone wrong, to make sure they know you're right—who's watching? Who's keeping score?

Most people, if they're honest, imagine some kind of panel. Some invisible audience tallying up wins and losses. Some cosmic accountant tracking whether you let people disrespect you or whether you stood your ground.

Maybe it's your parents' voices in your head: "Don't let anyone push you around." Maybe it's your culture's programming: "Real men don't back down." Maybe it's your own internalized belief that backing down equals weakness, and weakness equals failure.

But those scorekeepers don't exist.

Your parents aren't watching every confrontation you have, grading whether you defended yourself properly. Your culture isn't keeping a tally of how many times you stood your ground versus how many times you let something go. Your future self isn't going to look back at your life and think, "I wish I had gotten into more arguments with strangers."

The imaginary panel isn't real.

When someone cuts you off in traffic and you feel the surge of "I can't let them get away with that"—because who exactly would let them "get away with it"? There's no traffic police scoring your response. There's no manhood council reviewing whether you defended your lane properly. There's no cosmic justice system awarding points for standing up to inconsiderate drivers.

The scorekeeper you're imagining—the one judging whether you're being too passive, too aggressive, too weak, too confrontational—exists only in your head.

And the wild thing is, even though you know intellectually that nobody's actually grading you, you still feel the pull. You still feel like there's something at stake. Like if you let this go, you're losing some invisible game.

That feeling is real. The game is not.

The question isn't "How do I win?" The question is "Do I want to play a game that only exists in my imagination while risking things that actually exist in reality?"

You Don't Have to Win Everything

You can visit the Disney Parks without having to ride ALL the rides.

Seriously. You can go to Disney, ride three rides, eat some food, watch a parade, and go home. You don't have to maximize every minute. You don't have to hit every attraction. You don't have to "win" Disney.

But people try. They plan military-precision itineraries. They wake up at dawn. They power-walk between attractions. They skip meals to fit in more rides. They stress their families out trying to extract maximum value from their ticket price.

And then they go home exhausted, sunburned, broke, and barely able to remember what they actually enjoyed because they were so busy optimizing.

Life is the same way.

You don't have to engage with every idiot. You don't have to fight every battle. You don't have to defend your honor in every confrontation. You don't have to correct every person who's wrong on the internet.

You can just... let it go (pun intended).

Let them be wrong. Let them have the lane. Let them say stupid things at the game. Let them cut you off. Let them think they "won."

There is no scoreboard.

Nobody's tracking how many arguments you won. Nobody's grading you on how effectively you defended your team's honor. Nobody's giving you points for being right.

You're competing in a game that doesn't exist.

Beating the ETA

When was the last time you tried to beat the Estimated Time Arrival (ETA) from the GPS app?

Even if it's just 1 minute earlier, we won! Right? We beat the system!

Except you didn't. You merged aggressively into other drivers. You may have made their commute angrier. You may have risked an accident. And for what? To arrive 60 seconds sooner.

Nobody is grading how many times you beat your estimated time arrival.

I even subconsciously guardrailed myself about this in 2018 when I bought my car. It's a Prius C. It's not even possible to drive recklessly in this car. Coming from a Mini Cooper, this felt like: hey, you can (and you just can) drive peacefully.

Not that I'm driving at 20 mph now. But I'm not at 60 mph anymore. And the ETA from the GPS can stay the same or even go up. Nobody cares. There's no exam grading my arrival time.

That's what imaginary competition looks like on the highway: racing against an arbitrary number that doesn't actually matter, creating stress and risk for yourself and others, all to "win" something that was never a competition.

The Imaginary Leaderboard

Have you ever played a game like *Candy Crush*?

It's designed to be addictive. You beat a level. You feel good. You see your friends' scores. Some of them are ahead of you. So you play another level. And another. And another.

And then you realize you're spending money on a free game. You're losing sleep. You're ignoring your family. You're stressed about... *Candy Crush*.

For what? To be #1 on a leaderboard that literally doesn't matter?

Your best friend or your kids aren't going to remember you as "the person who was really good at *Candy Crush*." Nobody's going to carve "Top 10 in *Candy Crush*" on your tombstone.

But we treat real-life confrontations the same way.

We risk our jobs, our relationships, our freedom, our health—all to climb an imaginary leaderboard. All to prove we're better, smarter, more right than some stranger we'll never see again.

We act like there's a cosmic scoreboard tracking every argument we won, every person we put in their place, every time we defended our honor.

There isn't.

Stop Fighting Imaginary Battles

There's no teacher reviewing your life decisions and tallying up how many times you stood your ground versus how many times you let things go.

There's no cosmic report card at the end measuring whether you defended your honor properly, whether you let people disrespect you, whether you proved you were right often enough.

There's just the life you're actually living. The safety you're maintaining. The relationships you're preserving.

When you're lying in a hospital bed because a stadium fight went wrong, the doctor isn't going to hand you the "You Were Right" certificate. When you're dealing with the legal fallout from a road rage incident, the judge won't award you bonus points for being technically correct about the traffic violation.

The only measurements that actually matter are:

Are you safe?

Are the people you love safe?

Is this confrontation worth what you might lose?

That's it. That's the whole question. And you already know the answers.

The stranger at the stadium doesn't matter. The driver who cut you off doesn't matter. The person on the internet who's wrong doesn't matter.

What matters is getting home to your family. What matters is waking up tomorrow without a criminal record. What matters is not throwing away everything you've built for the temporary satisfaction of proving a point to someone who won't remember you five minutes from now.

So stop fighting battles that don't matter. Stop risking everything for nothing.

There is no exam. There never was.

The only grade that counts is whether you protected what actually matters while letting go of what doesn't.

And that's a test you can pass simply by walking away.

FIRST PIT STOP

We've been driving for a while now. Five chapters, actually.

You've merged onto the highway. Realized you're your own reference point. Met all those different versions of yourself that passengers see. Recognized the cultural viruses you've been carrying. Watched everyone perform their lives instead of living them. Confronted a grading system that never existed in the first place.

So let's pull over for a moment. Find a rest area. Turn off the engine. Step out and stretch your legs.

Look how far we've come from your neighborhood. When we started, you were on familiar side streets where everything made sense because you'd driven those routes a thousand times. Now we're on the highway, and things look different from here.

The cars around you aren't threats to beat anymore—they're just driving at their own speeds. The lane isn't yours to own. And all those rules you thought you had to follow? Most of them were just inherited ideas, not actual requirements.

You've seen how much of what you believed was true was just programming. Beliefs about needing to be first. Ideas about owning your lane. The assumption that someone's grading your performance. The pressure to keep up with everyone around you.

None of that was real. It was just learned.

We're about to get back on the road, but the next stretch is different. We're taking the scenic route now—the one that shows you how everything changes depending on where you're standing.

Ready to see how everything looks different from this viewpoint?

Let's go.

Part Three

THE SCENIC ROUTE

Taking the scenic route, seeing everything's relative.

Chapter 6

SPEED IS RELATIVE

I'm taking you on the scenic route now—not the highway where you're focused on speed and getting ahead. The scenic route is where you slow down and actually look around. You notice the landscape. The trees, the mountains, the other cars with people living their own lives.

That's what this part of the journey is about. Slowing down to really observe your surroundings—the people around you, the way you see everything. Not to change where you are, but to understand what you're actually looking at from where you stand. You have a unique view of the landscape because no one else is standing in the same spot as you.

And that includes how you see the other drivers—and let's be honest, not all of them look like geniuses out there.

There are people stupider than you, and people smarter than you.

Stupidity is relative to YOU. People are either smarter or dumber than you. That's just how our perception works.

Let's go back to the highway example. When you're cruising at 65 mph, the car going 80 mph looks reckless. The car going 50 mph looks incompetent. But neither of those observations is objective—they're both relative to YOUR speed. You're the zero point. Everything else is measured as "faster than me" or "slower than me."

Ever notice a car in your rearview mirror staying the same distance behind you for miles during a road trip? You immediately feel a connection with that driver—they're using your pace, they're driving like you. That empathy happens automatically because they match your speed. They feel "right" to you.

Intelligence works the same way. You're the baseline. People who understand things faster than you, who see patterns you miss, who grasp concepts that confuse you—they're "smart" relative to you. People who take longer to understand, who miss obvious patterns, who struggle with concepts that seem simple to you—they're "stupid" relative to you.

The Mental Ranking Line

Your brain does this automatically. Without you even realizing it, you've subconsciously ranked them in your head—an imaginary line of persons stretching to the horizon, all arranged by intelligence relative to you.

You're standing in your position on that line. Everyone you've ever met is sorted somewhere on it. People ahead of you are "smarter." People behind you are "stupider." Not universally—just relative to your interaction with them.

But what we struggle to realize: you can't move people forward on YOUR line. That person who seems stupid to you? You can't educate them to be smarter than you. You can't fix them. You can't explain things better until they suddenly rank higher on your line. They're positioned where they are based on how your brain interacts with theirs.

The line is fixed relative to you.

But—and this is crucial—that same person exists on everyone else's line too. And on their best friend's line? They might be way ahead. The person you ranked as "stupid" might be the most brilliant person in someone else's world.

So when you're tempted to "fix" or "educate" someone you've ranked behind you on your line, remember: you're not measuring universal intelligence. You're measuring their position relative to YOUR reference point. And that measurement has nothing to do with their position on anyone else's line.

You can't fix people who are behind you on your line. And you don't need to, because they're not universally behind—they're just behind relative to your perception.

The driver who cut into your path? You won't fix him by honking harder.

Stupid people are everywhere, and that will never change.

You can't fix them. You can't educate them. You can't force them to see reason. You can't make them admit they're wrong.

And more importantly, you're not being graded on how many stupid people you correct.

There's no teacher grading your life thinking, "Wow, look at how effectively they're putting idiots in their place. A+ for them!"

Let them be wrong. Let them cut you off. Let them say dumb things at the game. Let them have fun. Let them be stupid on the internet. Let them exist in their wrongness without making it your problem.

You're Also on Someone Else's Line

While you're busy ranking everyone on YOUR line, everyone in your life has their own line. Your parents had theirs. If you have kids, they have theirs. If you have a partner, they have theirs.

And you're on all of them.

Think about that. Your kids aren't comparing you to other parents. You ARE their reference point for 'parent.' You're their zero. You're the standard against which all other parents get measured on their line —not because you're competing with them, but because you're literally their baseline.

If you have a partner, they're not ranking you against other partners. You're the reference point for "partner" in their world. When they meet someone else's spouse, they might notice differences—"oh, they're more patient" or "they're less organized"—but those observations are measurements relative to YOU. You're the zero point. You're not in competition with those other spouses. You're the standard.

Therefore, trying to be awarded "the best" parent or "the best" partner is impossible. You're not competing in a race. You're not trying to rank higher than other parents or spouses. You're already their reference point. You're already the zero on their line.

The relief? You're not falling into someone else's reference line. Your kid's friend isn't thinking about you at all. Their friend's dad is THEIR reference point. You exist on their line somewhere, maybe ahead, maybe behind, but you're not their zero. You're not their standard.

Stop trying to compete with other parents or partners. You're not in that race. You're already someone's reference point. And they're not grading you against everyone else—they're measuring everyone else against you.

That's not pressure. That's liberation.

We Say Someone's "Right" When They Agree with Us

Ever notice how the people who think like you are "rational" and "logical," but people who disagree with you are "delusional" or "naïve"?

That's not because you have access to objective truth. That's because you're measuring their opinion against yours.

When someone agrees with you, your brain says, "Yes, this person is correctly aligned with the truth (which happens to be my position)." When someone disagrees, your brain says, "This person is incorrectly aligned with the truth (which is still my position)."

You're not evaluating their argument on its merits. You're evaluating how closely it matches your existing beliefs. And they're doing the exact same thing to you.

Take political views, for example. Whatever side you're on, the other side isn't just wrong—they're dangerously wrong. Delusional. Destroying the country. How can they not see what's so obvious to you?

And here's the irony: I didn't even mention which country, which flags, or political party I'm talking about. But you already mapped this onto your own political landscape, didn't you? Because this pattern exists everywhere. Every country thinks their political division is uniquely toxic, uniquely frustrating, uniquely impossible to bridge. "Our politics are broken," we all say, as if we invented polarization.

We all think our situation is special. But the mechanism is identical across borders: you're measuring everyone's political position against yours. The people who match your position are "informed." The people who don't are "brainwashed." And they're doing the exact same measurement from their reference point.

Remember the car in your mirror matching your pace? You felt that connection because they were driving like you. People who think like you feel the same way—"right" because they match your speed, your rhythm, your reference point. Both of you think you're right. Both of you think the other person is wrong. Both of you are measuring from your own reference point and acting like it's universal.

It's not. It's just yours.

Everything Measurable Is Relative

So if everything is relative to your position—intelligence, agreement, perception—what about the things we think are objective? Like wealth? Like beauty?

Let's test the relativity principle:

Who's richer—a homeless person with a penny in their pocket and zero debt, or a middle-class person with $50,000 in debt?

Objectively, the homeless person has a higher net worth. One penny is more than negative fifty thousand dollars. On paper, they're "richer."

But we don't think of it that way, do we? Because we're not measuring wealth objectively. We're measuring it relative to social position, access to resources, quality of life, security. The middle-class person has debt, sure, but they also have a home, food, healthcare access, job prospects. The homeless person has one penny and nowhere to sleep tonight.

So when we say someone is "rich" or "poor," we're not actually talking about numbers. We're talking about how their situation compares to our baseline expectation of normal.

If you grew up in poverty, making $50,000 a year feels rich. If you grew up in wealth, making $50,000 feels like a failure. Same number, completely different feeling, entirely dependent on where YOU started.

Being rich is relative. Always has been.

Beauty and Attraction

Same principle applies to beauty. You know what you find attractive—but where did that standard come from? Part of it is biological (we're wired to find certain things attractive—soft skin, symmetry, signs of health), part of it is cultural (what your society values), and part of it is personal (what feels familiar, what reminds you of positive experiences).

But here's what most people don't realize: your standard of beauty is based on YOU, on your face, on your body.

You are your own reference point for attractiveness. The features you have become the baseline for what feels "right" and attractive to you.

This is why people often partner with people who look similar to them. Not identical, but similar. Similar facial structures, similar coloring, similar proportions.

It's not a coincidence. You're unconsciously attracted to people who resemble you because they match your internal standard of beauty —which was built around your own features. You see yourself in the mirror every day. These features become familiar, comfortable, "correct." And when you see those features reflected in someone else? Your brain registers them as attractive.

There's a phenomenon where couples often look like they could be related, called assortative mating. Same general build. Similar facial features. Similar coloring. It's not because they've been together so long they've morphed into each other. It's because they selected each other in the first place based on physical familiarity.

You're attracted to your own reflection more than you realize.

When you see someone whose features echo yours—similar eye shape, similar nose, similar jaw line—they feel "right" to you. They match the standard you've been building your entire life by looking at your own face.

This isn't narcissism. It's just how reference points work. You are your zero point for beauty, just like you're your zero point for intelligence and speed and everything else.

Same principle extends to pets. People pick dogs that look like them. Or act like them. Or both.

It's not always obvious—you're not deliberately looking for a dog that matches your face. But subconsciously, you're drawn to the dog whose appearance or temperament feels familiar. Feels like... you.

You see a dog with your energy level, your facial structure (proportionally), your coloring—and something clicks. That dog feels "right." That dog matches your internal standards.

Relativity again. You're the standard, and you're drawn to what matches that standard.

When You're Not Happy with Your Own Standard

So what happens when you don't like your reference point? When you look in the mirror and wish you looked different?

That's where body modification comes in. Plastic surgery, hair transplants, implants, lifts, tucks, injections—all the ways people try to change their baseline.

And that's completely fine. Your body, your choice.

But there's a crucial question you need to answer before you modify: are you doing this for you, or for someone else?

Because if you're doing it for someone else, you're not actually changing your body. You're changing yourself to meet someone else's standard. And that never ends well.

The Modification Traps

You see someone famous with a specific look. They're successful, they're attractive, they're everywhere. And you think: if I looked like that, my life would be better.

But hold on.

That celebrity NEEDS that look. Their career depends literally on maintaining that appearance. They're paid to look that way. They have teams of people helping them maintain it. Stylists, trainers, nutritionists, surgeons. Their job is looking like that.

Your job isn't.

You don't get paid to look like them. You don't have their team. You don't have their income to maintain that appearance. And more importantly—you don't have their specific career that requires that specific look.

So if you modify your body to look like them, you're taking on all the costs and maintenance of their professional appearance... without any of the professional benefits.

You're cosplaying someone else's career requirements in your regular life.

Now, to meet someone else's standard?

Maybe you're thinking: "But if I change this one thing about my appearance, I'll finally attract the kind of person I want."

Stop.

If someone isn't attracted to you before the modification, but they are attracted to you after... what are they actually attracted to?

The modification. Not you.

They're attracted to what you changed to become for them. They're attracted to the fact that you bent yourself to meet their standard.

And now you're trapped in a relationship where the foundation is: you modified yourself to be acceptable to them.

Think about what that means in the long term. If your body changes naturally—aging, weight fluctuation, life happening—will they still be attracted? Or will they want you to modify again to keep up with their standard? Or will they look for someone else with those characteristics?

You've trained them to love something other than who you actually are.

Think about what that means: if someone only loves you AFTER the modification, they don't love you. They love what you became to please them.

They love the artificial result. The altered version. The you that bent to meet their standard.

And now you're stuck. Because if you ever stop maintaining that modification—if your body changes, if you age, if you can't keep up the appearance—will they still love you? Or will their attraction fade because the thing they were actually attracted to is gone?

You've built a relationship on a foundation of physical modification to meet someone else's standard. That's not love. That's a transaction.

Do It for Yourself, or Don't Do It at All

Modify your body if and only if YOU want to. For YOUR reasons. Because YOU genuinely want to look different or feel different in a way that serves your own life.

Not to look like someone famous who needs that appearance for their career.

Not to finally attract someone who wasn't attracted to the real you.

Not to meet someone else's standard of what you "should" look like.

Because if you do it for them, you're not changing your body—you're changing who you are for external validation. And that validation will never be enough, because it's not actually about you.

Your body. Your choice. Your reasons.

Not theirs.

Look, I'm a strong advocate for this because I've actually done it. I had a hair transplant a few months ago (or "hair relocation" as I jokingly call it—they're just moving your own hair from one part of your head to another). I did it to fix my receding hairline, and it went great. I feel amazing.

But here's the key: I did it for me. Not because someone said I should. Not to look like anyone else. I did it because I wanted to.

That's the only reason that matters.

What If Everyone Disappeared?

Here's a thought experiment that exposes how absurd external comparison is:

Imagine everyone else on Earth disappeared overnight. Pandemic, apocalypse, rapture—doesn't matter. You're the only person left.

Suddenly, you're the smartest person alive. And the dumbest. You're the richest and the poorest. The most attractive and the least attractive. The fastest and the slowest.

All the rankings disappear because there's no one left to compare yourself to.

Would you still care about being "the best"?

If you're the only person alive, does it matter that you can't run as fast as someone who no longer exists? Does it matter that you're not as smart as the people who are gone? Does it matter that you don't have as much money as people who aren't there to have money?

Of course not.

So why does it matter now?

The other people are still effectively invisible to your actual daily progress. Their existence doesn't change your capabilities. Their achievements don't diminish your growth.

You're competing in a race where the other runners won't even know you're on the track. And winning that race doesn't change your odometer—it just feeds your ego.

Compare yourself to yourself. Yesterday's you is the only person who had your exact circumstances, your exact resources, your exact challenges. Yesterday's you is the only person whose progress you can actually measure against, because you have complete data.

Did you move forward from where you were yesterday? Yes? Then you're progressing. Did you stay the same or move backward? Then you have information about what to adjust.

That's it. That's the whole measurement system.

Everyone else's progress is irrelevant to yours. You don't know their starting point. You don't know their advantages or disadvantages. You don't know what "forward" even means for their unique route.

But you know yours. You know where you were yesterday. You know where you are today. You know if you're moving in the direction you actually want to go. That's the only measurement that matters.

Einstein figured out that space and time are relative—they change depending on your position and speed. There's no absolute reference frame. Everything is measured relative to the observer. Two people traveling at different speeds experience time differently. Neither is "wrong." Both are correct in their reference frames.

There's no absolute standard for success, intelligence, beauty, or progress. There's just your reference frame and everyone else's reference frames.

Stop trying to jump into someone else's frame and measure yourself by their coordinates. You can't. You're always measuring from where YOU are.

So, measure your progress against your own position. Yesterday's coordinates compared to today's coordinates.

Your Odometer Is Yours Alone

Remember: your odometer measures distance traveled, not speed achieved. It measures cumulative experience, not competitive ranking.

Some people's odometers read higher numbers because they've been driving longer. Some read lower numbers because they started later. Some have traveled the same distance but on completely different roads.

None of that changes YOUR mileage.

You could be at 10,000 miles or 100,000 miles—the only thing that matters is whether today's number is higher than yesterday's.

Are you moving forward on your own route? That's success.

Are you driving at a pace that works for the road you're on? That's progress.

Are you comparing your odometer to your own previous reading instead of someone else's? That's wisdom.

There is no exam grading whether your mileage matches someone else's expected timeline.

There's just your odometer, your route, and the choice to keep moving forward.

Chapter 7

THEIR RIDE, YOUR MEMORY

L ook in the mirror, look at the road behind you. All those miles you've traveled—exits you took, rest stops, stretches of highway, cities you passed through.

What do YOU actually remember?

Maybe a particular sunset. Maybe that time you got caught in a rainstorm. Maybe the playlist you had on repeat for three hundred miles.

Now ask the person who was riding shotgun what they remember from that same trip.

Completely different details. Different moments. Different highlights.

Same road. Same car. Same miles traveled. Totally different memories.

You Want to Create Memories

All the time, we plan experiences specifically to create memories.

The perfect vacation route. The scenic detour. The special restaurant stop. The surprise destination. We carefully orchestrate every detail because we want the people with us to remember this trip forever. We're constantly seeking advice for a road trip—the perfect itinerary, the must-see stops, the optimal timing.

Why? Because we think there's an exam. We think we're being graded on how good of a host we are, how well we facilitated the experience, whether we created the "perfect" memory for them.

And we think if we plan it well enough, if we hit all the right stops, if we time everything perfectly—we can create the memory we want them to have.

The reality? Control can sometimes be an illusion. You control the route. You control the stops. You control the timing.

But... you don't control how the other person will experience it.

You're even planning based on how you think you would experience it—putting yourself in their shoes. But that only works for you relative to your experiences, your reference point. They have their own. What would thrill you might bore them. What you'd find meaningful might not register for them at all.

Your kid might remember the scenic overlook you drove two hours out of the way to reach. Or they might remember the argument about ice cream that happened before the overlook.

Your partner might remember the surprise destination. Or they might remember you being stressed about directions the entire way there.

Your friend might remember the perfect timing of arriving at sunset. Or they might remember needing to use the bathroom for the last hour and being too uncomfortable to enjoy the view.

What do they actually remember? They remember what caught their attention, what mattered to them in that moment, what their brain decided was worth keeping. Often something you didn't even notice—a weird billboard, a song on the radio, the way the light hit the dashboard. Sometimes something you wish they'd forget—the wrong turn, the closed restaurant, the GPS argument.

You planned the experience. They built the memory. And what they built might have nothing to do with what you planned.

Siblings Always Remember Different Trips

Ask siblings about a family road trip they all took together.

I've done it myself. My sister remembers it one way. I remembered it completely differently. Same car. Same parents. Same route. Same stops. Everyone was there.

Ask them and listen to their stories.

One remembers it as the best trip ever—laughing in the backseat, playing car games, eating snacks, feeling excited about the destination. Another remembers being bored and restless, stuck in the middle seat, constantly asking, "Are we there yet?" and being told to be quiet. Another barely remembers the trip at all—they had a book and read the entire way, tuning out everything else.

Who's right?

All of them. And none of them.

Memory isn't a video camera recording objective truth. Memory is a reconstruction. Your brain takes fragments—images, emotions, sensations—and builds a story from them every time you remember. And the story changes depending on what you need it to mean right now.

The sibling who remembers the trip as amazing might have been in a great mood that day, or maybe they desperately needed a good family memory and their brain gave them one. The bored sibling might have been going through something hard that week, and the car ride became another thing to endure. The reading sibling found their own escape, and that's what they needed.

Same experience. Three completely distinct memories. All real. All true for the person who has them.

How We Tend to Plan for the Future

Planning has a built-in limitation: we always plan with what we have in mind right now. Our experiences. Our reference point. Our current understanding.

We think we're crafting a future scenario—imagining what will matter, what will work, what will be meaningful years from now. But zoom out on this concept and you realize: we're just using our current mindset and understanding of what's feasible right now.

We can't actually imagine the future. We can only imagine an improved version of the present.

Bear with me for a second—I'm about to zoom way out on this one.

Lets talk about how we design cars. Right now, we're building technology to make our current cars drive themselves. *Waymo* vehicles—they're "regular cars" with steering wheels, just controlled by computers instead of human hands. *Waymo* belongs to Google and are cars that are driven automatically by cameras.

That's our "future vision" using today's baseline. We have cars with steering wheels, so we add cameras that monitor every surrounding, calculate risks and routes into their smart systems so that they can use those steering wheels to drive themselves with no need of a person in the driving seat.

But the actual future? It may not have steering wheels at all. The car will be designed from the ground up to move autonomously. No driving wheel. No pedals. No controls for a human driver who isn't needed.

We can't imagine that car yet because we're still thinking "car with a robot driver" instead of "car as robot."

Our "futuristic" idea is just our present reality, slightly upgraded. The actual future will have a completely different baseline we can't picture yet because we don't have it now.

If today we're building humanoid robots, we imagine the future in twenty years will have... better humanoid robots. They're what we can imagine right now.

The actual future twenty years from now? Maybe it's pet-sized robots or pocket *minions* for your desk. Things we can't picture yet because we're not thinking in those terms today. We'll be looking forward to whatever comes next, not looking back at "those humanoid robots from twenty years ago."

So what we call "imagining the future" is really just imagining how our current present could be better. It's philosophical, but think about it: if you already have a "futuristic idea," that idea exists today. You have it. You can build it right now with today's technology and mindset.

It's impossible to think of an idea from ten years in the future because we don't know what we'll have by then.

In 2005, it would have been impossible to imagine a touch-based app for mobile phones. Not because people weren't creative enough—because the iPhone didn't exist yet. Our thoughts couldn't include "touch interface" as a baseline. That wasn't in our present context.

In 2015, try imagining AI-generated images and videos. You couldn't, because generative AI hadn't changed how we think about content creation yet. That wasn't part of the present we were building from.

Same thing with cars. Right now, we're building robots to drive our existing cars. That's our "future vision": take what we have (cars with steering wheels) and make them better (let computers use those controls).

The actual future isn't our present upgraded. It's something built on a completely different foundation we don't have access to yet. That's why it even makes us laugh today when we see futuristic videos of people from the 50s and 60s.

What This Means for Memory Creation

So when you're stressing about creating the right memories for your kids, or planning the perfect anniversary trip for your partner, or trying to give your elderly parents one last great vacation—understand this:

You're imagining what they'll remember using today's context. What you think matters now. What you believe will be meaningful based on your current understanding.

But when they're remembering this trip ten years from now? They'll have different contexts. Different priorities. Different needs from that memory.

You can't predict what will matter to them because you don't know who they'll be when they're doing the remembering.

Maybe the carefully planned scenic route becomes their favorite memory. Maybe it's the random gas station where you bought them a candy bar they'd been begging for all day. Maybe it's just the way you said "hello friend" when they got in the car. Maybe it's something you don't even remember happening.

You're planning with today's map, trying to predict what future-them will value. But you don't have their future map yet.

And this applies to everything you plan—not just road trips. When you plan a wedding, a birthday party, an anniversary celebration—you're not creating the same perfect event for everyone. You're facilitating an event that will trigger emotions and hopefully memories for everyone there (including you!).

Think of yourself as an "emotion facilitator". You're creating the environment where people can experience their own feelings, their own moments, their own potential memories. If you want to change things, perhaps you should try from within—changing the environment you control, not the memories they'll build.

You set the mood, choose the food, arrange the lighting, select the music, set the full ambiance. That's your goal. That's what you can control.

Everyone will attend a different party. What moves one person will bore another. What one guest remembers as the highlight of the night, another won't even notice. And that should be expected.

All you can do is drive. Be present on the journey. Create the environment. This only works if you let go, too. Trust that they'll find what they need from the experience.

Your Memory, Their Memory, Everyone's Memory

Memories are personal, and they exist for that person for a reason. They have a purpose, the way they're crafted in that person's mind, not necessarily the factual way. They're not objective recordings of what happened. They're subjective reconstructions built from fragments every time someone accesses them.

You can't control what other people remember about experiences you share. You can't force them to remember your version. You can't create their memories for them no matter how perfectly you plan the route.

You're all safe in that car together. All you can do is drive. Be as present as your brain allows (which, remember, is always somewhat in the future anyway). Make the trip. Trust each passenger will take what they need from it.

And when their memory contradicts yours? Let it. Their version is real for them just like your version is real for you. Neither is more "correct."

Stop trying to orchestrate perfect memories. Stop stressing about whether you're giving people the experiences they'll value later. Stop fact-checking the memories you already have.

Just drive.

You're not being graded on whether everyone remembers the same trip the same way. You're not being graded on whether the memories you tried to create match the memories that actually formed.

There is no exam measuring whether you created the "right" memories.

There's just the journey. And whatever each passenger builds from it.

That's their memory to construct. Not yours to control.

Chapter 8

YOUR ODOMETER, YOUR MILES

O n this stretch of highway, you'll notice something interesting: there are multiple routes to get to the same general area. Some drivers take the interstate—straight, fast, efficient. Others take the scenic route—winding, slower, more interesting. Some take back roads through small towns. Others stick to toll roads to avoid traffic.

They all work.

There's no objectively "correct" route. There's just the route that makes sense for your priorities, your vehicle, your timeline, your preferences.

But we've been taught to measure "success" as if there's only one valid route—the fastest one. The most direct one. The one that gets you there before everyone else gets there.

Except... where is "success"? And why does getting there first matter if you hated the entire drive?

Personal Success is Beating Uncertainty

What are you actually trying to accomplish when you pursue your personal "success"? You're trying to beat uncertainty.

Think about it. Why do you want money? To reduce the uncertainty of whether you can pay rent, buy food, handle emergencies. Why do you want a stable job? To reduce the uncertainty of where your next paycheck comes from. Why do you want good relationships? To reduce the uncertainty of being alone, unloved, unsupported.

Personal success isn't about having more than other people. It's about having enough to feel secure in your own life.

Everyone wants comfort. Everyone wants to reduce the anxiety that comes from not knowing if their basic needs will be met. But the amount of comfort you need to feel secure is relative to YOUR baseline, not someone else's.

Someone who grew up with food insecurity might feel successful the moment they have a full pantry and three months of rent saved. Someone who grew up wealthy might not feel successful until they have a vacation home and retirement fully funded.

Same word—success—completely different destinations. Neither is wrong. They're just operating from different starting points with different uncertainty thresholds.

You're not trying to beat other drivers. You're trying to beat your own uncertainty about whether you'll be okay.

The Scenic Route vs. the Interstate

Let's say you're driving from the city to the beach. You have options:

Route 1: Interstate

Direct, fast, boring. Gets you there in about 6 hours. Nothing to see except farmland and rest stops. Efficient, practical, optimized for speed.

Route 2: Pacific Coast Highway

Winding, slower, breathtaking. Gets you there in 10+ hours (more if you stop). Ocean views, bay vistas, cliffs, small coastal towns, photo opportunities. Scenic, memorable, epic, optimized for experience.

Which route is "successful"?

If you define success as "arriving fastest," the interstate is the express pass. If you define success as "enjoying the journey," the coastal route wins. If you define success as "not getting carsick on winding roads," maybe you avoid the coast entirely.

There's no universal metric that says one route is objectively better. There's just what matters to YOU on THIS trip.

Instead, you look at other drivers taking the interstate, see them arriving before you, and assume you failed because you took a different route. You measure your journey by their destination, their timeline, their priorities.

That's insane.

Your route was different because your goals were different. You weren't trying to get there fastest—you were trying to see the ocean. You weren't trying to minimize drive time—you were trying to maximize the experience.

Both routes end up in the beach. Both drivers "succeeded" at getting there. But if you spent the whole coastal drive stressed about not being on the interstate, you just ruined your own route by measuring it against someone else's.

Quality over Quantity

You're driving, getting hungry. Someone with you is searching on their phone for nearby restaurants and finds two options:

Restaurant A: 4.7 stars from 4,937 reviews

Restaurant B: 5.0 stars from 54 reviews

Which one is better?

Most people would say Restaurant A. They have nearly 5,000 people who thought the experience was worth reviewing. They've served exponentially more customers. They've scaled. They've reached more people. Just like you select a product on amazon.

But Restaurant B has a perfect rating. Every single person who reviewed it thought it was flawless. Maybe it's a tiny place that can only serve 20 people per night. Maybe the chef personally oversees every dish. Maybe they focus on creating one perfect experience at a time instead of maximizing volume.

Is Restaurant B worse because fewer people know about it? Or better because everyone who experiences it thinks it's perfect?

There's no objective answer. There's no "right" answer. It depends entirely on what you're measuring.

If you measure by reach and scale—Restaurant A wins. If you measure by consistency and quality—Restaurant B wins. If you measure by revenue—probably Restaurant A. If you measure by customer satisfaction—probably Restaurant B.

The point is: the metric you choose determines what "better" means. And every metric is relative (and let's be honest, arbitrary). There's no cosmic scoreboard that says, "Restaurant A is objectively better." There's just different ways of keeping score, and you get to choose which one matters to you.

But what happens? You don't choose. You let other people choose for you. You let culture tell you that scale equals success, or money equals success, or fame equals success. And then you spend your entire life optimizing for a metric you never actually wanted.

The Parental Competition Trap

Scroll through social media during report card season. See how many parents post about honor roll, awards, achievements.

"My daughter made the honor roll again!" "So proud of my son!" "Straight A's!" "Advanced placement classes here we come!"

Every post sounds like it's about the kid. But look closer—it's about the parent. The parent is competing through their child's achievements. The parent is using their kid's grades, activities, accomplishments as proof that they're a "successful" parent.

And it's not just grades. It's the shoes they wear to school. You buy little Lacoste shoes because you know they're classy and they signal you can afford quality—but maybe your kid just wants some Spider-Man shoes from a generic brand. Who are those Lacoste shoes really for?

What that kid absorbs: "My value is based on what I achieve and how I look. My worth is measured by how I perform and present compared to other kids."

That's not parenting. That's putting your child in a competition they didn't sign up for so you can claim the trophy when they win.

The really messed up part? The kid's grades don't actually make you a better or worse parent. Their test scores have nothing to do with whether you're raising a kind, resilient, happy human being.

You know what makes you a good parent? Being present. Listening. Showing them how to handle failure. Taking the walk with them when they need to talk. Teaching them that their worth isn't tied to their performance. Helping them find their own route instead of forcing them onto yours.

But we don't measure parenting that way, do we? We measure it by comparing kids. "My kid is reading at a higher level than yours" becomes code for "I'm a better parent than you."

It's the same competition trap, just with higher stakes. And the kid pays the price.

Don't Do Their Homework

For those competing through their kids' achievements, here's where it gets absurd: there are parents doing homework for their children.

I'm not talking about helping. I'm talking about doing. Writing their essays. Building their science projects. Solving their math problems.

Why? So the kid gets a better grade. So the teacher thinks the kid is smarter. So the kid gets into advanced classes. So the parent can post about it on social media.

But who actually learned something? Not the kid. The kid learned that someone else will do the work if the stakes are high enough. The kid learned that performance matters more than learning. The kid learned that they're not capable enough to do it themselves.

You just sabotaged your own child's education to win a competition that doesn't exist.

There is no exam grading whether your kid is smarter than someone else's kid. There's just your kid's actual education, which you just undermined by teaching them to fake competence instead of building real capability.

If your kid struggles with homework and fails the assignment, they learn something valuable: this subject is hard for me and I need to ask for help. I need to put in more effort, and I need to figure out where I'm confused.

If you do the homework for them and they get an A, they learn nothing except that performance is more important than growth.

Which outcome actually serves them better in life?

Your Destination Isn't Universal

(No, not talking about the park. Universal Studios is actually one of our favorite destinations.)

It comes down to this: there's no universal destination that everyone should drive toward.

Some people want the corner office. Some people want to work from home in their pajamas. Some people want to build a business. Some people want stability and predictability. Some people want adventure and risk. Your route is your own adventure.

None of those destinations are objectively "more successful" than the others. They're just different routes with different endpoints that appeal to different drivers.

But we've been taught to measure success as if everyone should drive to the same place. Like there's one correct destination—usually defined by money, status, or visibility—and everyone who ends up somewhere else failed to get there.

That's not how routes work.

You're driving YOUR route to YOUR destination based on YOUR priorities. Someone else taking a completely different highway isn't evidence that you're lost. They're just going somewhere else.

The guy who retired early to travel the world isn't more successful than the woman who built a company and works 60-hour weeks. A stay-at-home mom is just as successful as a woman who founded a company. The person who makes $50k doing work they love isn't less successful than the person making $200k doing work they barely tolerate.

They're just on different routes with different destinations and different ideas of what matters.

Success has no universal metric because there's no universal destination.

The Pressure to Perform

This is hard to internalize because everywhere you look, someone is trying to sell you their definition of success.

The university tells you that success means a degree from a prestigious school. The company tells you that success means climbing the corporate ladder. Social media tells you success means followers, likes, engagement. Your classmates tell you success means keeping up with their lifestyle.

Every direction you turn, someone is holding up a scoreboard and telling you that THIS metric is the one that matters. THIS destination is where you should be heading. THIS route is the correct one.

And if you're not optimizing for their metric, you're falling behind.

Except you're not falling behind. You're just not in their race.

You're on a different highway, heading toward a different destination, measuring progress by different landmarks. And that's exactly what you should do—as long as YOU chose the route instead of letting everyone else choose it for you.

What Do YOU Want?

The real question is: what do you actually want?

Not what your parents want for you. Not what society says you should want. Not what looks impressive on social media. Not what your classmates are chasing.

YOU. What do YOU want?

If money weren't a measure of success, what would be? If nobody was watching or judging, what route would you take? If you couldn't compare your journey to anyone else's, what destination would matter to you?

Those questions are hard to answer because you've been trained to measure success externally. You look at what other people have, what other people have achieved, what other people are doing—and you use that as the definition of success.

But their route isn't your route. Their destination isn't your destination. Their metrics aren't your metrics.

You need to figure out what success means to YOU. Not to your parents, not to your culture, not to Instagram. To you.

And then you need to drive toward that destination without constantly checking your rearview mirror to see if you're keeping up with the cars around you.

Which means you'll probably need to unlearn what you've been told.

The Odometer, Not the Scoreboard

Remember: your odometer measures YOUR miles traveled on YOUR route. It doesn't compare you to other drivers. It doesn't rank you against everyone else. It just shows how far you've come from where you started.

So 10,000 miles toward a destination you actually chose is more fulfilling than 50,000 miles toward a destination everyone else chose for you.

You can't fail at someone else's definition of success. You can only fail to pursue your own.

So stop measuring your journey by their scoreboard. Stop comparing your scenic route to their interstate. Stop thinking you're behind just because they arrived somewhere before you did.

They arrived at their destination. You're still heading toward yours. And that's exactly how it should be.

There is no exam grading whether you chose the "right" route or the "correct" destination.

There's just your journey, your choices, and whether you're actually driving toward something that matters to you.

Part Four

REST AREA

Stepping aside from the road to unlearn old driving habits.

Chapter 9

STOP WATCHING OTHER LANES

V ery early in the journey, someone told you: "You must go faster. You need to be faster, better, first." And you believed them because everyone else did too.

Now you're at a rest area. Part Four of the journey. The unlearning stops.

This is where you get to pull over, open the trunk, and ask: "What have I been carrying? Do I still need all of this?"

Let's start with something you've carried for miles: the belief that you need to compete.

Competition Is Taught Everywhere

Think about it. Everything in life has trained you to compete.

School graded you against classmates. Sports rank your team against others. Work measured your performance on a curve. Even entertainment—the things you do to relax—became competitions.

Video games show leaderboards. Social media counts likes. Fitness apps compare your steps to everyone else's.

You can't even play Candy Crush without seeing that Susan is at level 389 while you're at 307. Now you're not enjoying the games. You're catching up.

To what? For what?

If you beat Susan to level 401, what do you win? Nothing. Not money, not status, not even Susan's respect because she probably isn't thinking about you at all. You win the knowledge that you're ahead on a scoreboard that only exists in your head.

That pattern didn't start with video games. You learned it way back in your hometown, probably before you could even drive. You learned that being first matters. Winning is everything. Falling behind means you're losing.

And you've been carrying that belief ever since—hundreds of miles down the highway, through dozens of towns, into completely unfamiliar territory.

Maybe it's time to pull over and ask: do you still need it?

Welcome to the Rest Area

You've been driving for a while now. You've left your hometown. You've merged onto the highway. You've seen how everything's relative, how memories belong to others, how success has no universal metric.

You've learned a lot about what's been weighing you down.

Now comes the part where you get to set some of it down.

Not because you were wrong to carry it. Not because you should've known better. But because you're allowed to travel lighter. You're allowed to look at what you packed back in your hometown and say, "I don't need this anymore."

Competition is one of those things.

You were told that competition was necessary. That it's how you survive, how you succeed, how you prove you matter. Everyone in your hometown believed it. Your parents believed it. Your teachers believed it. Your friends believed it. So you believed it too.

And it made sense back there. In that context. In that town where everyone measured themselves against everyone else, where every achievement was a ranking, where every success was relative to someone else's failure.

But you're not in that town anymore.

Look in your rearview mirror. That town is miles behind you. And yet you're still driving like you're navigating those old streets, still competing like you're back in that old race, still carrying that heavy belief that you need to beat everyone around you to matter.

You don't.

You can let that go now.

The Suitcase You've Been Carrying

Think of competition like a suitcase someone handed you when you left home. "You'll need this for the journey," they said. And you believed them because everyone else had one too.

But you're at a rest stop now. You can open that suitcase. Look at what's actually inside.

Maybe you find: the belief that being first means you're worthy. The anxiety of falling behind. The exhaustion of racing everyone around you. The habit of measuring your joy against someone else's disappointment. The fear that if you're not competing, you're giving up.

Well, there it is. None of that is improving your drive. None of that is helping you enjoy the route. None of that is necessary for where you're heading.

So why keep carrying it?

Not because you're bad for having it. Not because you should've dropped it sooner. But you can choose what comes with you to the next town. And competition? That can stay at the rest stop.

But What About Ambition?

So, what are you thinking? "If I stop competing, won't I lose my drive? Won't I fall behind? Won't I stop caring about improvement?"

No.

Unlearning competition doesn't mean you stop trying. It doesn't mean you stop growing. It doesn't mean you stop having goals.

It means you stop measuring your growth by how many people

you've passed. It means you stop defining success by whether you're ahead or behind. It means you stop letting other people's journeys determine the value of yours.

You'll still want to improve. But you'll be improving because you want to see how far you can go, not because you need to prove you're better than someone else.

You'll still set goals. But they'll be your goals, based on your destination, not someone else's idea of where you should be by now.

You'll still work hard. But you'll work toward something that actually matters to you, not toward staying ahead in a race you never signed up for.

The difference: you'll enjoy the drive.

What Unlearning Looks Like

It's not dramatic. It's not a single moment where everything clicks and you're suddenly free.

It's pulling over at rest stops like this one and asking: "What am I still carrying from my hometown? Do I need it for where I'm going?"

It's noticing when you're racing and choosing to drive instead.

It's catching yourself comparing and redirecting: "That's their route, not mine."

It's seeing your kid struggle—with homework, with friendships, with setbacks—and letting them navigate it. Not because you don't care, but because you care enough to let them build their own capabilities. It's not about control. It's a relationship based on respect.

Let them have their own journey. Let them succeed on their own terms. Let them fail and discover they can recover. That's life. That's how the journey works.

Their grades don't make you a better parent. Their achievements don't validate your choices. Their performance doesn't determine your worth.

You're their parent, not their scorekeeper. And the beautiful part? When you stop competing through them, they get to stop competing for you. They get to just be kids figuring out their own route.

That's not giving up on them. That's giving them space to drive by themselves.

The Path You're in Now

The highway you're on now doesn't work like your hometown. The rules are different here. The priorities are different here. What mattered back there doesn't need to matter here.

Back there, everyone raced. Everyone compared. Everyone measured their worth by their ranking. That's just what you did.

But you're in fresh territory now. You've passed through different towns. You've seen different ways of driving. You've learned that not everyone defines success the same way, that not everyone is heading to the same destination, that not everyone is racing.

Some people are just driving. Enjoying the route. Stopping when they want to stop. Going at their own pace.

And they seem... lighter. Less stressed. More present.

Maybe that's because they unpacked competition somewhere along the way. Maybe they stopped at a rest area like this one and said, "I don't need to carry this anymore."

You can do that too. And if you're worried you won't figure it out without the race—don't be. Your route finds a way.

You're Not Giving Up

The hardest part of unlearning competition is that it feels like quitting.

If you stop racing everyone around you, are you giving up? If you stop comparing your route to everyone else's, are you settling? If you stop measuring your worth by your ranking, are you losing ambition?

Nope.

You're just choosing to define progress differently. You're choosing to measure growth by your own standards instead of someone else's scorecard. You're choosing to enjoy the towns you're driving through instead of rushing past them to get ahead.

That's not giving up. That's waking up.

You've spent miles—maybe years—racing people who aren't even going to your destination. Comparing yourself to drivers on completely different routes. Stressing about being ahead or behind in a competition that only exists in your head.

What if you just... stopped?

What if you drove at a pace that felt right for you? What if you enjoyed the scenery instead of staring at the cars around you? What if you measured your day by whether you moved forward, not by whether you passed someone else?

You'd still get where you're going. You'd just enjoy the drive a lot more.

The Next Town Doesn't Require Competition

Look ahead. See that next town on the horizon?

You don't need competition to get there. You never did.

Competition was something your hometown taught you. It's not a law of the highway. It's not required on the journey. It's just a habit you picked up back there and kept doing because everyone else was doing it too.

But the highway is long. The route is yours. And you get to decide what you carry with you.

Some things from your hometown are worth keeping. Some lessons, some values, some habits—work well for you, they make the drive better, and they help you navigate. The past is a lesson, not a blueprint.

But competition? That's deadweight. That's the thing making you anxious when you should be enjoying the view. That's the thing turning every stretch of highway into a race you can't win.

You can leave it here.

Not with shame. Not with regret. Just with the simple recognition: "I don't need this for where I'm going."

Driving Forward

When you leave this rest stop, you'll still see other cars. You'll still notice some going faster, some going slower. That won't change.

What changes is what you do with that observation.

Instead of speeding up to pass them, you might just think: "They're going somewhere. I'm going somewhere. We're both traveling."

Instead of feeling behind, you might just think: "I'm exactly where I need to be on my route."

Instead of comparing your journey to theirs, you might just think: "I wonder where they're headed."

That's what unlearning competition looks like. Not dramatic. Not perfect. Just gradually letting go of the belief that you need to beat everyone around you to matter.

You matter because you're on your journey. Because you're driving your route. Because you're here, moving forward, making choices, navigating your life.

Not because you're ahead of anyone. Not because you're winning. Just because you're you, and your journey is yours.

There is no exam grading whether you kept up with traffic.

There's just your route, your choices, and the freedom to drive without racing everyone around you.

Welcome to this rest area. Stay as long as you need. And when you're ready, keep driving—lighter than before.

Chapter 10

THE HIGHWAY
BELONGS TO EVERYONE

E very kind and color of vehicle imaginable share this highway
with you.

Sedans and SUVs. Hybrids and electric cars. Cars that run on gas,
cars that run on diesel. Motorcycles weaving through lanes. Eighteen-
wheelers hauling cargo. RVs moving at their own pace. Manual transmissions, automatic transmissions, some vehicles you can't even
categorize.

Different engines. Different sizes. Different capabilities. Different
purposes.

And they all share the same highway.

The road doesn't ask what kind of engine you have before letting
you on. It doesn't require a specific transmission type. It doesn't
measure your fuel efficiency or judge your vehicle choice. The highway
accommodates everyone because the highway understands something
fundamental: we're all just trying to get somewhere.

Different vehicles. Same journey. Same right to travel safely.

The Suitcase You Didn't Pack Yourself

At your last rest stop, you unpacked competition. You looked at that heavy belief and said, "I don't need this anymore."

But there's another suitcase in your trunk. One you didn't even pack yourself. One that got loaded in before you started driving, back in your hometown, before you were old enough to question whether you wanted it.

It's labeled "division."

Inside, you'll find: the belief that some vehicles belong on the highway more than others. The habit of categorizing drivers into "us" and "them." The assumption that different means separate. The idea that diversity is something to tolerate rather than something that just... is.

None of that was your idea. You inherited it. Your hometown taught it. The surrounding culture reinforced it. You've been carrying it for so long you might not even notice it's there.

But you're at another rest stop now. You can open that suitcase too.

The One Race Reality

Look at what the evidence actually shows about individuals: we're only one race. We are the human race.

Not metaphorically. Not philosophically. Literally.

We're all the same species. Different expressions of the same blueprint. Different paint jobs on the same fundamental vehicle.

Neil deGrasse once asked a version of this cosmic query: when we imagine aliens, why do we always picture them with two arms, two legs, a head on top—basically humanoid? Look at Earth. We have fish, mollusks, insects, spiders, plants, fungi, mammals of every shape imaginable. Gazillions of life forms that don't possess the human shape at all.

So why would aliens look like us?

We imagine them that way because we're the reference point. We're so focused on our own shape that we assume intelligence, consciousness, advanced life must look like we do.

We already know diversity is the norm. We see it everywhere on Earth. And yet when it comes to humans? We act surprised that we all look basically the same. We create divisions based on minor variations —skin tone, eye shape, hair texture—when the reality is we're remarkably very similar. Just different shades of the same basic design.

Different skin tones aren't different races. They're just different colors of the same vehicle. Like cars coming off the same assembly line in different paint options. Blue, red, white, black—same car, different finish.

We already know this. As a matter of fact, we already accept this with other species.

Look at dogs. Billions of dogs. Millions within each breed. They come in every color combination imaginable—black, brown, white, spotted, striped. Do dogs care what color another dog's fur is? Do they judge each other based on coat color? Do they divide themselves into "us" and "them" based on whether they're golden or dark brown?

No, they're just dogs. Different colors of the same species. And they know it.

We're the same. Different colors of the same species. We just forgot to act like we know it.

The Border Crossing Paradox

Back in my hometown, I lived two hours from the border. I'd drive north into Texas regularly.

Same person. Same car. Same journey. But suddenly I had a new label when I crossed.

In Monterrey, I was just a person. In Texas, I was a PoC—a person of color, a term used in the United States to categorize anyone who isn't white. I'm part of a minority. Latino. Hispanic. Labels that didn't exist for me two hours south.

Nothing about me changed. I'm still me, in the same car, on the same highway. But the labels kept shifting based on where I was and who was doing the labeling.

But the divisions aren't real. They're just lines we drew on maps and then pretended define who people are.

I didn't cross a border and become a different species. I didn't suddenly transform into a different type of human. I was the same person I was two hours ago, driving the same route, with the same destination.

The division was invented. And if it was invented, it can be uninvented.

The *Doppelgänger* Truth

We're one species. Different expressions of the same blueprint, yes. But here's something interesting: with finite traits and 120 billion humans who have existed, lookalikes aren't just possible—they're kind of expected.

Think about it. Eye spacing, nose shape, cheekbone structure, jawline, hair texture—there are a lot of possible combinations, but it's still a finite number. When you have 120 billion versions of the species cycling through those combinations, the chances are high that certain sets of traits will repeat.

We point at them because they look so weird—like a person from 200 years ago just reincarnated—but mathematically, it's almost inevitable.

You may have seen those photos: celebrities who look identical to historical figures from decades or centuries ago. Enzo Ferrari and Mesut Özil, separated by decades, practically twins. Actors who look exactly like people from old photographs. Strangers on the internet who could be siblings but have never met.

We act surprised at this. "Wow, they look so similar!"

But why are we surprised? We're all crafted with the same basic features, just mixed in different proportions.

Dogs look identical without being related. Same with cats. Same as any species with a large population. Limited combinations with finite traits means you're going to get repeats.

We're not that different from each other. We never were. We're all variations on the same theme, built from the same blueprint, driving the same kinds of vehicles on the same highway.

The divisions we see? We were taught to see them. They're not built into reality. They're built into the way we learned to look at reality.

Different Conditions, Same Species

Some people are extroverts. Some are introverts. Some are straight. Some are gay. Some are left-handed. Some are autistic. Some are tall. Some are short. Some are loud. Some are quiet.

Different conditions. Different preferences. Different ways of being.

Same species. Same highway. Same right to drive their own route.

Supporting people in living their lives with joy and authenticity shouldn't be political or controversial: it's just human. We are here to give others the same space we want for ourselves.

If someone a thousand miles away believes in a different religion than you and that makes them happy, how does that impact your life? Why would you want to force them to believe in the same religion that you do? If someone expresses their gender differently than you express yours, how does that change your route? If someone's brain works differently than yours, processes the world differently, finds joy in different things—how does that affect where you're going?

It doesn't.

They're driving their vehicle. You're driving yours. You're both on the same highway, heading to different destinations, living different lives that don't actually intersect except for the shared road beneath you.

And if you're worried that your kid might learn something from another car—something you don't want them to learn—start inside your own car. Make you the example. Be the driver they're watching. Your kid is in your vehicle, seeing how you navigate, how you treat other drivers, how you respond to differences on the highway.

They're learning from your driving, not from the cars passing by.

The division—the belief that their different route somehow threatens or diminishes yours—that's something your hometown taught you. That's something you've been carrying in your trunk, taking up space, adding weight, making your drive heavier than it needs to be.

You can unpack that now.

The Highway Doesn't Discriminate

The highway accommodates all vehicles because the highway isn't invested in your differences. It's just a road. It holds the weight of sedans and semi-trucks in the same way. It lets motorcycles go fast and RVs go slow without judging either.

The highway works because it's designed for diversity, not uniformity.

Imagine if the highway only accommodated one type of vehicle. Only sedans allowed. If you're driving a truck? Too bad, find another route. Motorcycle? Not welcome here. Electric car? We support only gas engines.

That would be absurd. The highway would be empty. Half the vehicles would sit on side roads, unable to get where they need to go, because the road decided their differences disqualified them.

That's what division does. It takes a highway designed to accommodate everyone and turns it into a restricted route where only certain vehicles are "allowed." Not because those vehicles are inherently better. Just because someone decided to draw arbitrary lines about who belongs.

The highway doesn't care what you're driving. It just cares that you're traveling safely, sharing the road, not trying to run other vehicles off just because they look different from yours.

Maybe the car you're judging right now because it looks different is the one that would stop to help you miles ahead when you get a flat tire. Maybe you're in traffic right now, surrounded by vehicles, but that car would be the only one near you on a stretch of highway miles away from the city. Now it will spot you, and you'll be the one calling out for help.

So, if your car breaks down and needs a fuel "transfusion," you won't turn down help because the other driver's chassis doesn't match yours or because they are playing Lady Gaga on their radio. You just need what keeps you alive on the road.

The Proximity Perspective

Simon Sinek, one of my favorite authors, famous for the book *Start With Why*, and an advocate of the *Infinite Game* mindset—which this book flourishes on and is built upon—tells a story about how proximity influences connection. Let me frame it this way:

Your neighbor. The one who lives across the street.

If you see him on your street, you might wave. You might not. Depends on the day. He's just another person in your neighborhood.

If you see the same neighbor in another city—completely unexpected—you stop. "Hey! What are you doing here?" You chat for a couple of minutes. Exchange pleasantries. Then, you both go on your way.

If you see him in another country, holy shit! In a place where they speak a distinct language? Where everything feels foreign? You WILL reach out. You'll talk for a long time. You make plans. You found a familiar face (familiar as in now he's family, huh?), someone who speaks your language.

Now imagine you're an astronaut. You get sent to the International Space Station. When you arrive, you see your neighbor there. No fucking way!

Suddenly he becomes the most important person in your life.

The same guy you wouldn't even wave to across the street? Up there, millions of miles from Earth, he's the most important person in your life. You're both floating in space together. Context makes him your brother.

Now take it further: imagine the person you hate. The one who roots for the opposing team. The one with completely opposite political views. The one you avoid at family gatherings.

If both of you get assigned to a mission on the ISS, wouldn't you leave your differences aside?

Up there, you're not opponents. You're the most similar species out there. Not the most different—the most similar. Because everyone else is millions of miles away on Earth.

The further away you are, the more the sameness matters. The closer you are to home, the easier it is to focus on differences.

When you're in your neighborhood, surrounded by familiarity, divisions feel important. But put yourself far away—in another country, on a space station, millions of miles from Earth—and suddenly those divisions disappear. You just see people. Fellow humans. Drivers on the same highway.

When Labels Matter

In the 1800s, being a left-handed was seen as witchcraft. Sorcery. Something wrong with you. Some parents would tie children's left hands behind their backs to force them to use their right hand. Schools would punish kids for writing with the "wrong" hand.

Today? Nobody cares whether you're left-handed or right-handed.

The label only matters in specific contexts. If you're a football coach trying to protect your quarterback's blind side, knowing whether he's a lefty or righty matters. That label in that context makes sense.

But for everyday purposes? It's irrelevant. You don't see celebrities announcing, "Hey everyone, I gather the media here today for this special announcement, I want you to know—I'm a lefty!" You don't see news coverage of someone "coming out" as left-handed.

That same principle applies to everything we treat as divisions: sexual orientation, gender identity, religion, neurodivergence, cultural background. The labels might matter in specific contexts—medical contexts, social contexts, legal contexts—where they need to be acknowledged and protected.

But for everyday interaction? For whether someone deserves respect, dignity, space to drive their own route? The labels are as irrelevant as being left-handed.

The Three Steps

I think the journey toward true non-division (a.k.a. being inclusive) follows these steps:

1. Awareness: Recognizing that differences exist and are common. This worked out since the 1800s for lefties. Understanding that neurodiversity exists. That people have different orientations. That 8+ billion people means 8+ billion different expressions of being human.
2. Acceptance: Understanding why someone might be different—why they have different tastes, why they need quiet, why they react strongly to change, why they express themselves differently—and adapting to be more inclusive. Not just tolerating, but actually making space.
3. Indifference (the positive kind): Reaching a point where these differences are just another natural human variation. Like being left-handed is today. Not something you need to comment on, celebrate, or criticize. Just... part of how humans are.

We can't force step 2. We can't make people accept what they aren't ready to accept. But we can absolutely champion step 1—awareness. We can point out that we're all on the same highway, driving different vehicles, and that's just how highways work.

And if enough people reach awareness? Acceptance follows. And indifference—the kind where nobody cares who you love or how you think or what makes you different because we're all just people trying to get somewhere—that becomes the natural consequence. Full circle. From "different" back to "just people."

The 8 Billion Realities

If you're an advocate of labels, if you need to put a label on each different person to categorize them properly, you're going to end up with 8 billion labels.

Because every person is a different person.

Not even identical twins are the same person. They're living proof that you can look exactly the same and still be two completely different people inside. They're often opposites in terms of behavior, preferences, personalities.

Everyone is different. So why do we always want everyone to be the same?

Why do we want everyone to think the same? To have the same political beliefs as us? The same religious views? To like the same things, watch the same movies, go to the same temple to pray—or to be agnostic like we are?

Why do we expect everyone to have the same capabilities, the same mentality, the same approach to life?

We're 8+ billion different (living) expressions of the same species. Different vehicles on the same highway. And yet we spend so much energy trying to force everyone into the same category, the same lane, the same route.

That's not how highways work. That's not how species work.

You're Allowed to Let This Go

Division might feel like something you need to protect. Something that keeps you safe. Something that helps you navigate.

But look at what it actually does: it makes you suspicious of other drivers. It makes you see threats where there aren't any. It makes you waste energy categorizing people instead of just driving your route. It turns every interaction into an evaluation: are they like me or not like me? Can I trust them, or should I be worried?

That's exhausting. That's anxious. That's not making your drive better.

You don't have to get along with everyone. You don't have to be around people who think completely different from you. They're driving their route. You're driving yours. The highway accommodates you both without requiring you to drive together.

There's a reason there are several lanes.

You're allowed to let that go. You're allowed to see other vehicles as just... other vehicles. Different from yours, sure. But sharing the same road, trying to get somewhere, dealing with the same traffic and weather and construction zones you're dealing with.

Not threats. Not competition. Just other travelers on the same highway.

You don't have to carry division anymore. It was handed to you in your hometown. You've been hauling it around for miles. But you're at a rest stop now. You can leave it here.

Not because you were wrong to have it. Not because you should have known better. But because you're allowed to travel lighter. Because the next town you're heading toward? It doesn't require you to divide people into categories before you're allowed in.

You can just drive. And let other people drive too.

What Changes When You Unlearn Division

When you leave this rest stop without that suitcase, here's what changes:

You stop seeing "us" vs. "them." You see people.

You stop categorizing drivers by their vehicle type. You recognize they're on journeys just like you are.

You stop feeling threatened by differences. You see them as just... different expressions of the same thing.

You stop wasting energy policing who belongs on the highway. You focus on your own route, your own destination, your own drive.

That's not naive. That's not ignoring real problems. That's just choosing to see reality clearly: we're all the same species, driving the same highway, trying to get somewhere that matters to us.

Different vehicles. Different routes. Different destinations. Same fundamental right to make the journey.

There is no exam grading who is rooting for the best political view or religion.

There's just the highway, accommodating every vehicle, and your choice about whether you drive with division weighing you down or with the lightness of knowing we're all just people trying to get somewhere.

Welcome to this rest area. Unpack that suitcase. Leave the division behind.

And when you're ready, keep driving—toward a town where everyone's allowed on the road.

Chapter 11

THEIR MAP ISN'T YOURS

Y ou're not driving the same route as anyone else. You didn't start at the same place. You're not heading to the same destination. Your vehicle isn't the same. Your passengers aren't the same. Your constraints aren't the same.

So when someone tells you, "If this worked for me, you should do it," what they're actually giving you is directions from their starting point to their destination, in their vehicle, under their conditions.

That's the thing about advice—it always comes with an invisible context. How many times have you given advice? We share diets, careers, parenting strategies, productivity hacks, relationship advice with absolute certainty. Someone finds something that works in their life and immediately wants to share it—genuinely, enthusiastically, convinced it's the answer.

And sometimes it is. For them. In their context. With their vehicle, on their roads, with their specific passengers and constraints.

The advice trap isn't taking advice. It's forgetting that all advice comes with an invisible asterisk: it worked in my specific situation.

The Origin You Can't See

When someone gives you advice, they're sharing directions from their hometown to their destination. They know every street sign, every traffic pattern, every shortcut. What they can't see is that you're not starting from their hometown—you're starting from yours.

Their advice makes perfect sense. For someone leaving from their location, with their vehicle, headed where they're going.

The trap is assuming their route will work from your starting point.

Think about driving directions. If someone tells you, "Turn left at the big oak tree on your right," that's only helpful if you're approaching from the same direction they were. From a different angle, you might not see the oak tree at all. Or you'll see three oak trees. Or maybe the oak tree was cut down last year, but they haven't driven that route since.

Their directions aren't wrong. They're just not universal.

The Suitcase Full of Someone Else's Context

Every piece of advice comes packed with context. Their job situation, their family structure, their personality, their financial position, their health, their values, their fears, their experiences. All of it invisible to you, built into their recommendation like a suitcase you can't see.

Someone tells you to wake up at 5 a.m. because it changed their life. What they don't mention: they're morning people, the don't have kids, they go to bed at 9 p.m., they work from home, and they love having quiet time before the world wakes up. They even share videos on social media of their morning routines with timestamps that don't include the time they took to set up the camera.

You try it. You're a night owl, you have a toddler who wakes up twice a night, your commute starts at 7 a.m., and you do your best thinking after 10 p.m.

Their advice was real. Your context is different. The advice doesn't transfer.

Someone recommends that you quit your job and follow your passion like they did. What's invisible in that advice: they had six months of savings, a supportive partner with stable income, no kids, good health insurance through their spouse, and a marketable skill they'd already been developing on weekends.

You have three months of rent saved, you're the primary earner, you have two dependents, and your passion is something that takes years to monetize.

Their advice wasn't wrong in their situation. It might be catastrophic for yours.

The Rest Stop Realization

Examine the advice you've been carrying. Not to reject it, but to understand where it came from.

That productivity system that makes you feel guilty because you can't maintain it? It was designed by someone with different energy levels, different responsibilities, different brain chemistry than yours.

That relationship advice that never seems to work? It came from someone in a different type of relationship, with different communication styles, different histories, different needs.

That parenting strategy that makes you feel you're failing? It was written by someone with different kids, different resources, different support systems.

None of this makes the advice bad. It makes the advice contextual.

The Disney Trip Thought Experiment

Someone watches and criticizes a family for having a rigid schedule at Disney—every ride planned, every meal timed, every photo spot mapped out. "They're too stressed! They should just relax and enjoy it!"

But what that critic can't see: maybe that family saved for years for this trip. Maybe this is their only chance to go. Maybe having a plan means they'll actually get to experience everything they saved for instead of wandering around overwhelmed. Maybe the parents genuinely enjoy planning—that organization isn't stress for them. It's how they have fun.

The critic's advice ("just relax!") comes from their context: maybe they live close enough to visit regularly, maybe they have annual passes, maybe spontaneity is how they enjoy things.

Neither approach is wrong. They're different vehicles on different journeys.

The advice trap is thinking your way of doing Disney (or anything else) should work for everyone.

What "Fun" Actually Means

Ask ten people what a "fun weekend" looks like and you'll get ten completely different answers:

Someone who works from home might want to get dressed up and go somewhere loud and social.

Someone who works in retail might want to stay home in pajamas and see absolutely no one.

Someone who sits at a desk all day might want to go hiking.

Someone who's on their feet all week might want to lie on the couch and binge a series.

When any of these people say, "You should try this, it's so fun!"— they mean it's fun for someone with their energy, their preferences, their context. They're not wrong. They're contextual.

The trap is hearing "you should" as if it's a universal prescription instead of "this worked from my starting point."

Stop Following Someone Else's GPS

Your GPS is programmed for YOUR destination. Not theirs.

Someone tells you, "You need to network more to advance your career." That might be true if you're in sales, if you're extroverted, if you're in an industry where relationships drive opportunities.

It might be completely wrong if you're in a field where your work speaks for itself, if you're building something that takes years of focused solo effort, if you advance through expertise rather than connections.

Their GPS isn't lying. It's just not calibrated for your route.

Someone says, "You need to save 20% of your income." That's solid advice if you make enough that 20% is possible, if you don't have debt crushing you, if you don't have dependents relying on you, if you don't have medical expenses eating your paycheck.

It's useless advice if you're barely covering rent.

The advice itself isn't bad. The context is everything.

Role Models vs. Imitation

You can look at how someone else drives and get inspired. You can notice their technique, their composure, their efficiency. You can learn from watching them.

What you can't do is replicate their exact route when you're starting from a different location.

Role models work when you take the principles and adapt them to your context. Imitation fails when you try to copy the exact moves from their context into yours.

Someone built a successful business working 80-hour weeks. They never give up. You can admire their dedication without destroying your health trying to match their schedule when you have different energy, different family needs, different life stages.

Someone achieved something through aggressive networking and constant hustle. You can respect their approach without forcing yourself into a style that drains you when deep work and careful thinking is your actual strength.

Look for inspiration, not imitation. Take what resonates and leave what doesn't.

You were taught that successful people wake up early, so you should too. You were taught that you need to hustle constantly, so you feel guilty resting. You were taught that there's one right way to raise kids, to manage money, to advance your career.

All of that advice came from someone's context. Some of it might transfer to yours. Most of it won't, at least not exactly.

The trap is treating context-specific advice as universal law.

Yes, Including This Book

Everything in this book—every metaphor, every suggestion, every observation—came from my context. My vehicle, my roads, my passengers.

Something might resonate with your situation. Something might not apply at all. Something might need to be adapted significantly to work for your commute.

This isn't advice. It's perspective. It's how things look from where I'm driving, with the understanding that you're driving from somewhere else.

If the driving metaphor helps you think about your journey differently—take it with you. If it feels forced or doesn't match how you see your life—forget it.

The trap would be me telling you, "This worked for me, so you should do it." The actual message is, "This is what I see from my seat. Take what makes sense from yours."

When You Picture Your Own Driveway

Someone asks on a Reddit community you belong because of the car you own: "Just bought the same car model you all drive—any tips for handling it?"

You type advice based on your experience: watch the tight turning radius in parking garages. The blind spot on the passenger side needs extra attention. Keep it in sport mode on the highway for better response.

All genuinely helpful. For someone driving your routes.

But what you can't see: they live on a farm in the middle of nowhere. No parking garages. No highway commutes. Their "blind spot concerns" involve livestock, not lane changes. Your sport mode advice is useless when they're navigating dirt roads at 15 mph.

You weren't wrong. You were contextual.

This happens constantly.

Career advice from someone who entered their field when jobs were plentiful and education was affordable—applied to someone entering the same field now when the landscape is completely different.

Relationship advice from someone who met their partner at 22—given to someone who's building a relationship at 42 with completely different life experience.

Parenting advice from someone raising kids before smartphones existed—applied to someone navigating digital childhood.

Financial advice from someone who bought their first house when they cost three times annual salary—given to someone when they cost ten times annual salary.

The advice was real. The context was different. Your city driving tips don't help someone on a farm.

What Advice Actually Means

When someone says, "If this worked for me, you should do it," what they actually mean is:

"This worked in my vehicle, on my roads, with my passengers, given my constraints, with my personality, at my life stage, in my circumstances."

They just don't say all that because they can't see it. Their context is water to a fish—it's everywhere, so it's invisible.

Your job isn't to reject their advice. Your job is to translate it.

Ask yourself:

What was their starting point?

What's my starting point?

What constraints were they working under?

What constraints am I working with?

What worked for them in their context?

What would that principle look like in my context?

Sometimes the answer is, "This translates directly—I can use this."

Sometimes it's, "This doesn't apply to my situation at all."

Most often it's, "I can take the principle and adapt it to my route."

The Permission You Didn't Know You Needed

You have permission to take the pieces of advice that resonate and leave the parts that don't.

You have permission to adapt what works for them into something different that works for you.

You have permission to say, "That's great that worked for you, but my context is different." Loyalty to someone else's advice won't help you if that advice doesn't fit your context.

You have permission to take someone's advice—even from a close friend—and tweak it to fit your situation. And if they notice and get defensive: "Hey, you didn't follow my advice!", you have permission to say: "Yes, I did. I adapted it to my context. It's totally your recipe, just adjusted for my kitchen."

You have permission to stop feeling guilty for not following advice that doesn't fit your situation.

You have permission to stop comparing your route to someone else's when you're starting from different locations.

The advice trap is thinking that if something worked for them, it should work for you exactly as they did it.

The exit from that trap is understanding that all advice is contextual—and your job is to filter it through your reality, not force your reality to match their advice.

Take what translates. Adapt what's close. Leave what doesn't fit. The time is now to stop following someone else's GPS.

There is no exam grading whether you followed someone's advice correctly.

There's just your context, your constraints, and whether you're driving a route that actually makes sense for your journey.

Chapter 12

EVERY TURN GOT YOU HERE

Of all the turns you could have made, you made the ones that got you here.

Every intersection. Every decision about which lane to take, which exit to choose, which route to follow. You made thousands of them. And each one brought you to this exact spot, reading this exact sentence, in this exact version of your life.

You can't hit Ctrl-Z, go back and drive a different route. Those other routes are no longer there. They may exist in some parallel universe where a different version of you made different choices. But that is not your universe. That's not your journey.

This is.

Here's the shift: there's nothing to regret. Not because you should "let go" of regret or "forgive yourself" for past choices. But the concept of regret shouldn't apply to your life.

There were no wrong turns. There were only the turns that brought you here, alive, now.

This might be the heaviest unlearning yet. This is heavy. Regret feels so justified. So earned. So obvious.

You took routes you "shouldn't have." You made choices that led to pain. You wasted time going in the "wrong" direction. How can there be nothing to regret?

Simple, those routes weren't wrong. They were the only routes that led to you being here right now. And "here right now" means you have the criteria you have now. The maturity. The wisdom. The mileage on your odometer.

That's not nothing. That's everything.

The Tree That Shows Your Path

Imagine a tree. A massive tree with thousands of branches spreading in every direction.

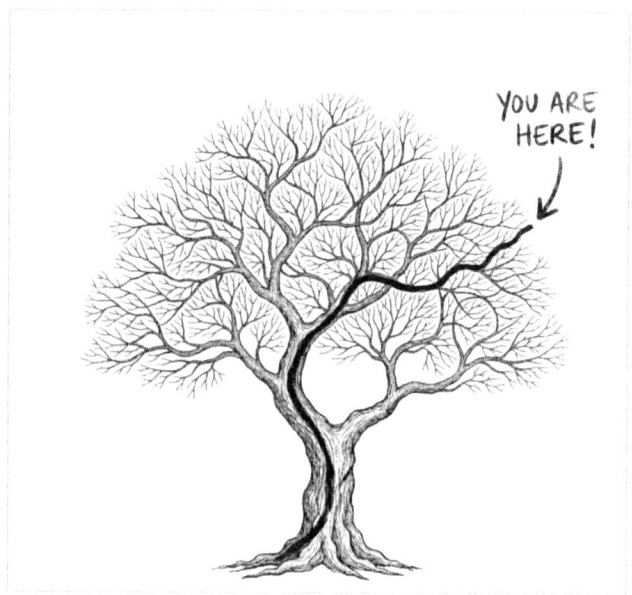

At the bottom is the trunk—your origin, where you started.

At the top of one specific branch, there's a black legend that says, "You Are Here!"

There's a thick line that traces one continuous path from the trunk to where you are now. One route through thousands of possible branches. One path that brought you to this moment.

Look at all these other branches. Thousands of them. Each one represents a choice you didn't make. A different path that a different version of you might have taken.

These branches are real. They exist on the tree. But they're not YOUR set of branches. They're not part of your path.

Your path is the black line. One continuous route from trunk to tip. Every turn, every intersection, every choice—they're all part of that single line.

You can look at the other branches and think "what if." You can imagine what might have happened if you'd taken a different route five years ago, ten years ago, twenty years ago.

You can't be on a different branch and still be you.

Because you are the black line. You are the sum of every choice that created this specific path through the tree.

If you'd chosen differently at any point, you wouldn't be you anymore. You'd be a different version. Living on a distinct branch. With a different path. A different life.

Not a better life. Not a worse life. Just different. Unknowable.

The Only Version That Exists

In quantum physics, there's this concept that every choice creates a branching universe. You chose left, and somewhere a parallel universe exists where you chose right. Both versions of you exist, living different lives.

That's a fascinating thought experiment in physics.

It's completely irrelevant to your actual life (this version, the one reading this book).

Because you don't live in multiple universes. You live in this one. On this branch. Following this black line.

That other version of you, who turned left instead of right? Who took the job instead of turning it down? Who stayed instead of leaving?

They don't exist in your reality. They exist in theory. In imagination. In the "what if" scenarios you replay at 2 a.m. when you can't sleep.

You exist here. Now. On this branch.

And this branch is the only one that matters because it's the only one that's real for you.

The Same Route, Never the Same Drive

Think about a road trip you've driven multiple times. Same starting point. Same destination. Same highway.

It's never identical.

This time you decide to stop for a bio break at mile 150. Last time you stopped at mile 175.

You pass a slow-moving truck, get ahead of it. Your family wants snacks, so you pull into a rest stop shop.

While you're inside buying drinks, you look out the window and see the same truck you passed rolling by on the highway.

"Oh not again," you think. Now you'll have to pass them again. But you might not encounter them again at all.

Maybe they're taking an exit a mile up the road that you're not going to take. Maybe they're stopping at the next gas station and you're not. Maybe you'll pass them again, maybe you won't.

Same route. Different variables. Different timing. Different outcome.

You can't recreate a journey, even when you're trying to. Too many variables. Too many other drivers making their own choices. Too many minor differences in timing cascade into completely unique experiences.

So when you imagine going back and "redoing" a choice from five years ago—taking the other job, staying in that relationship, moving to that other city—you're not just imagining a different choice. You're imagining an impossible scenario where everything else stays the same except for that one decision.

But that's not how it works. Change one choice, and everything changes. Every subsequent intersection. Every person you meet. Every opportunity that appears or disappears. Every version of who you become.

You can't redo your path and get a better outcome.

The path you're on is the only one that's real. And it's the only one that brought you here.

You may have heard this *cliché* question: "If you had a time machine and you could travel back 25 years and just say one thing to your younger self, what would you say?"

People love answering this. "Lottery numbers." "Bitcoin." "Don't date that person." "Take that job." "Avoid that mistake."

That's regret.

My message to my younger self would be: "Describe how you see yourself in 25 years."

That's it. Obviously I will silently laugh and enjoy his (my) response because younger Eric has no idea of what's snowballing ahead.

I wouldn't warn him about anything because if he takes a different turn anywhere, this version of me is gone. I vanish from my family photos. I didn't end up marrying Silvana. My son doesn't exist. The person writing this book never existed. Why would I want to do that?

Your Choices Define Your Life

If the combinations in our DNA define our living self, the combinations of our choices define our life.

You are not just the person with this specific genetic code. You are the person who made these specific choices, in this specific order, under these specific circumstances.

Those choices built your path. Choice by choice. Turn by turn. Intersection by intersection.

And that path led to you being here, with the understanding you have now.

There's a line from a TV series—*Prime Target* on Apple TV+—that fits here, where one character says: "We all have choices. What I've learned is that it's the ones we make that define us."

Not the choices we wish we'd made. Not the choices other people think we should have made. Not the theoretical choices that would have led to different outcomes.

The choices we actually made.

You are not the person who would have made different choices. You are the person who made these choices.

That's your life.

There Are No Wrong Choices

This is where it gets deep.

You think some of your choices were wrong. You regret them. You wish you could go back and choose differently.

But what "wrong" implies is that there was a right choice you should have made instead.

There is no exam grading your choices. There's no universal standard for "right" decisions. There's no scorecard measuring whether you chose correctly.

Think about the job you hated. The one you regret taking. The one that felt like two years wasted.

Was it the wrong choice?

What if that job made you resilient? What if it taught you to endure difficulty? What if it clarified what you absolutely don't want in life? What if it put you in the same room as someone who became crucial to your path later? What if it gave you skills you didn't know you needed?

What if—and this is the critical part—what if turning down that job would have led to a branch where you're not here right now?

You don't know what would have happened on the other branch. You can't know. That branch doesn't exist for you.

What you know is this: the choice you made led to you being here. Still on your journey.

That's not a wrong choice. That's the only choice that led to this outcome.

The "What If" Trap

"What if I had stayed in that relationship?" "What if I had taken that job offer?" "What if I had moved to that city?" "What if I had started that business?" "What if I had gone to that other school?"

What if. What if. What if.

When you play the "what if" game, you imagine a scenario where you made a different choice and everything turned out better.

But that's not how branches work.

If you'd stayed in that relationship, you don't just get the good parts of staying. You get an entirely different path. Different conflicts. Different growth. Different challenges. Different version of you.

Maybe that version is thriving. Maybe that version is miserable. Maybe that version isn't alive.

You don't know. You can't know.

What you know is that the choice you made—to leave—led to you being here. And "here" means you're still on your branch, still driving, still making choices with everything you've learned so far.

The "what if" trap makes you think you can see the other branches clearly. That you know what would have happened if you'd chosen differently.

You can't. Those branches are fog. They're imagination. They're stories you tell yourself at 2 a.m. about paths you didn't take.

Your branch is the only one that's real. And it's the only one that brought you here.

To Put It Cold: You're Alive

Let's strip away all the philosophy and get to the core truth.

Every choice you made led to you being alive right now.

Every "wrong turn." Every "mistake." Every decision you regret. Every path that felt like it was leading nowhere.

All of them led to you being here. Breathing. Reading this. Still driving forward.

You don't know what would have happened on the other branches. Maybe they led to better outcomes. Maybe they led to worse. Maybe they led to you not being here at all.

That means every choice you made was the right choice for this version of you. Not because it led to the best possible outcome. But because it led to this outcome: you, here, still driving.

There is no exam grading whether your path was optimal. There's only your path, and it got you here.

The Perfect Parents for Your Route

"I have the best mother in the world.—I have the best father in the world."

We all say this. Not because we objectively measured all parents, and ours scored highest. But because our parents are our reference point for "parent." They're our zero on that line.

They're not necessarily the best objectively. They're the best for your route. Because they're the only parents who planted and water YOUR specific tree.

Think about it: your parents were the first major split in your branches. The trunk. The foundation of every choice that came after.

With different parents, you'd be a different person. Not better. Not worse. Just different. Completely different.

Different parents would have taught you different lessons—or not taught you at all. They would have provided different resources, different support, different challenges. They would have created different circumstances that led to different choices that led to different branches.

And none of those branches would be yours.

Your parents—these specific people, with their specific strengths and flaws and presence or absence—shaped YOUR specific route. Even the setbacks. Even the absence. Even the moments when they weren't there when you needed them most.

Those weren't deviations from the "right" upbringing. Those were the exact ingredients that created you.

They taught you how to drive. Maybe they taught you poorly. Maybe they taught you perfectly. Maybe they left you to figure it out on your own. Doesn't matter. Their teaching—or lack of teaching—created YOUR driving style. Your approach to the road.

You can't wish for different driving lessons without becoming a different driver entirely.

Even parents who caused harm, who were absent, who made

terrible choices—they still shaped the branch you're on. You can acknowledge the pain they caused. You can recognize the ways they failed. You can choose not to repeat their patterns.

But you can't regret that they were your parents without regretting your entire tree. Because different parents = different you. Not the version of you that's reading this. A different version on a distinct branch that doesn't exist in your reality.

Your parents were perfect for you. Not because they were flawless. Not because they didn't make mistakes. Not because you're required to thank them or forgive them or maintain relationships with them if they were harmful.

But because they created the version of you that exists. This version. The one on this branch, with this path, with this specific 100% of life.

Say it out loud: "I had the best mother in the world.—I had the best father in the world."

Because they were yours. On your route. The only parents who could have created the you that's here now.

Everyone has "the best parents in the world" on their own route. Because everyone's parents created the specific branch that specific person is on.

That's not gratitude required. That's just reality.

Your parents were the first turn on your route. You can't wish for different first turns without wishing to be on a completely different route—which would make you someone else entirely.

And you're here. This version. On this branch. That's the only version that exists in your reality.

What "Wrong Turn" Really Means

When you say a choice was a "wrong turn," what you're really saying is: "I didn't like where that choice led me."

Okay. Fair. Some paths are hard. Some choices lead to pain. Some routes take you through territory you never wanted to see.

But calling it "wrong" implies there was a correct choice you should have made instead. And the correct choice would have led to a better outcome.

And what you're missing: you don't know if that's true.

You're comparing the actual path you took to an imaginary path you think would have been better. But that imaginary path is just that —imaginary.

The actual path? It taught you. It made you resilient. It showed you what you're capable of enduring. It revealed your values. It built your strength.

And it got you here.

That's not a wrong turn. That's part of your route.

You didn't make wrong choices. You made the only choices that the circumstances at that moment led you to make, consciously or unconsciously.

Forgiveness Doesn't Change the Past, But It Does Change the Future

You've likely heard this expression used when discussing self-forgiveness.

That's beside the point.

What changes your future is forgiving other people. The driver who cut you off. The friend who betrayed you. The person who hurt you.

Holding on to anger at them doesn't change what happened. But it ruins your future drive. It makes you bitter. It makes you drive with rage instead of peace.

You won't forget. You'll think twice if the same scenario repeats itself. But you'll forgive to move on.

Forgiving them sometimes not because they deserve it, but because you deserve to stop carrying their weight. That's what changes the future.

By the way, I'm not saying you should only forgive and never apologize because they should just forget. When you hurt someone, you need to ask for forgiveness—even if the harm wasn't intentional. And don't hide behind the empty line "I'm sorry that my actions hurt you."

Take ownership: "I'm sorry I hurt you, even if I didn't realize it at the time."

What You're Unlearning

You're not unlearning how to carry regret.

You're unlearning the belief that regret applies to your life.

You were taught that some choices are mistakes. That you should feel bad about wrong turns. That regretting past decisions is natural and justified.

But look at your path. Look at the black line from trunk to tip.

Every choice on that line brought you here. Every turn was necessary to create this specific version of you.

That thing you regret—not explaining something properly when someone asked you a question? That turned you into the teacher you are now that explains everything with detail. That relationship that ended badly? That taught you what you actually need in a partner. That job you hated? That clarified your non-negotiables. That friendship you lost? That showed you the difference between convenience and connection.

All of that crafted your life and your purpose. Those aren't mistakes to regret. They're the building blocks of who you are right now.

Don't strip that away from you.

There are no mistakes on your path. Because every choice was the only choice that led forward.

You can't regret a choice that was the only path to you being alive now.

That's not justification. That's just reality.

The Miles You've Driven

Your odometer records every mile you've traveled. It doesn't label some miles as "good" and others as "wasted." It doesn't judge which routes were optimal.

It just counts. Forward. Always forward.

Even when you drive in reverse, it counted those miles. Even when you took detours, it counted those miles. Even when you got lost, it counted those miles.

They all count. They're all part of your journey.

You can look at your odometer and say, "I wish I hadn't driven those miles." But those miles are still there. They still happened. You can't go back in time and delete them. They're still part of your total distance traveled.

And they brought you here.

You're not defined by having driven the "right" route. You're defined by having driven this route. Your route. The only route that's real for you.

The Only Branch That Matters

When you leave this rest stop, you're not erasing your past. You're not claiming you wouldn't choose differently if you could do it over.

You're just recognizing reality: you can't do it over. Those other branches don't exist for you. And the branch you're on—this one, the real one—is the only one that brought you here.

Every choice you made was the only path forward that led to this moment.

Not because you made the obvious choices. Because you made the choices you could make, in the moments you had to make them, with the information and emotions and constraints you were working with.

And those choices built your path. One continuous line from where you started to where you are now.

You exist on this branch. Not because it was the best branch. Because it's the only real branch that DEFINES you.

There is no exam grading whether you took a "right" path.

There's just your path, your choices, and what they brought you here.

You are here. On your branch. Alive!

That's not a consolation prize. That's a realization. That's everything.

And when you're ready, keep driving—not lighter because you dropped regret, but clearer because you finally understand it was never yours to carry.

SECOND PIT STOP

That was heavy terrain. Four rest areas back-to-back—four chapters of active unlearning.

Competition. Division. Advice. Regret. You just drove through some of the densest mental territory on this journey. Part Four asked you to unpack beliefs you've been carrying for miles—beliefs about needing to win, needing to follow someone else's route, needing to separate yourself from other travelers, needing to regret the turns you made.

That's a lot.

So now let's pull into a pit stop for a quick breather.

Rest areas have garbage cans for a reason. You've been examining what you're carrying. You've been deciding what still works for you and what doesn't. And now you get to throw away what you don't need anymore.

The competition? Toss it.

The belief that advice should fit you perfectly without translation? Toss it.

The habit of dividing people into categories before you even see them? Toss it.

The regret about turns that were the only path forward to you being here? Toss it.

You don't need to carry that weight into the next part of your journey.

Take a moment. Stretch. Process what you just worked through.

Part Four was about unlearning—actively letting go of programming that was never yours to begin with. It required pulling over, opening the trunk, and deciding what to keep and what to leave behind.

You did that work. That matters.

Ready to get back on the road?

Part Five is different. You're heading back into traffic—rush hour, actually. All the other vehicles around you, all those other travelers on the highway.

But now? Now you can actually see them.

Not as obstacles. Not a competition. Not as categories to sort them into.

As people. As fellow travelers. Each one the center of their own journey, just like you're the center of yours.

Part Four lightened your load. Part Five shows you what happens when you drive without that weight.

Let's go.

Part Five

RUSH HOUR

Back in traffic, but now seeing everyone differently.

Chapter 13

DRIVERS, NOT OBSTACLES

U ntil this moment, have you ever really looked at the driver in the car in front of you?

Not just glanced. Actually looked.

Noticed they're probably listening to music you can't hear. Maybe singing along. Maybe they're late for something important. Maybe they just got good news. Maybe terrible news. Maybe they're thinking about an argument they had this morning, or planning what to say at a meeting this afternoon, or wondering if they remembered to turn off the stove.

They have a whole life happening inside that car. A complete existence with worries and hopes and people waiting for them and problems to solve and memories that make them smile and wounds that still hurt.

But you don't see any of that.

You see: car in front of you. Going too slow. Obstacle.

Welcome to Part Five: Rush Hour

You've pulled out of those rest areas. You've done the heavy unlearning

—competition, advice traps, regret, division. You've examined what you were carrying and decided what to keep and what to throw away.

Now you're back on the highway. Back in traffic. Rush hour.

But something's different now. Because after all that internal work, you can finally see something you couldn't see before. We've got to think differently.

The other drivers aren't obstacles. They're not background scenery. They're not traffic statistics.

They're people.

Full people. With complete lives that are just as real and complex and important to them as yours is to you.

This is the shift from seeing characters around your story to seeing co-characters in their stories alongside yours.

The NPC Reality

If you've ever played or watched a video game, you've seen them. The characters that populate the world around the main character.

The sheriff standing outside the police station. You walk up, press X, and he delivers his line. The sorcerer in the tent who sells you that weird potion you'll need three levels later. The pedestrians walking down the street who aren't going anywhere—they're just there to make the city feel alive. Background movement. Scenery.

In video game terminology, these are called NPCs—Non-Playable Characters. You can't control them. You can't be them. They exist to support your mission or fill the space around you as you move through the game world.

That's how we naturally perceive most people we encounter during our day.

The person in line at the supermarket. The driver three cars ahead. The cashier scanning your groceries. The stranger walking past you at the mall.

It's almost impossible to simultaneously hold the awareness that every single person you pass has a complete life. People are overlooked for a variety of biased reasons—not that we're fully selfish (though some of us are sometimes). That they're the center of their own life just like you're the center of yours. That they're also thinking about buying gifts for their sons, saving for a vacation, worrying about whether they remembered to lock the door, just waiting to get home after their shift to take care of their folks.

The barista making your coffee isn't just a coffee-making function. The driver going too slow isn't just an obstacle between you and your destination. The customer service rep on the phone isn't just a voice solving or spinning around your problem.

But that's how they feel. Like NPCs in your game.

And we don't just see them that way. We treat them in that way.

When Everyone's Waiting in a Tent

Think about the last time you made a service appointment. Hair salon. Car repair. Doctor's office. Dentist.

You schedule it. You get the confirmation. And then life happens—traffic is worse than you expected, a meeting runs long, you can't find parking. You're running fifteen minutes late.

You feel a little stressed about it. Maybe a little apologetic when you finally walk in.

But deep down? You're not that worried. And sometimes not even for them, but for you not to portray yourself as an unpunctual person. Because somewhere in your mind, they were waiting for you anyway.

Like the video game sorcerer in the tent we were talking about. You're wandering through the forest for twenty minutes, you find the hidden clearing and you enter the mysterious tent, and there he is. Sitting there. Waiting. With the exact same greeting every time you visit.

"Ah, I've been expecting you."

Of course he has. He's an NPC. He exists in that tent, waiting for you to need him. He doesn't have other customers. He doesn't have a life that continues when you're not there. When you leave the tent and the screen fades, he's just... frozen there. Waiting for your next visit.

That's how we subconsciously think about service workers without even realizing it.

Of course the hairstylist isn't thinking about their next client or trying to stay on schedule. They're just... there. Waiting for you. The mechanic doesn't have three other cars to work on today. The doctor's office staff doesn't have a packed waiting room and people running behind and insurance companies to call.

They're in their tent. Waiting.

Except they're not. They have four other appointments today. They have a lunch break they're trying to protect. They have a daughter they need to pick up from school at 3 p.m. They have their own stress about running behind because the last customer showed up late too.

But you don't see that. Can't see that. Because in your story, they're the NPC who appeared when you needed them.

Next time you drive to work or to the supermarket, just pick any quick 10-15 minute drive. During that period, don't think about other people's lives—just count how many people you see in total. People ahead of you, around you at a traffic light. Forget about their lives and just count the number of people you see. Now reflect on the number at your destination. Was it 5? 10? 20? 50? And that was just a 10-minute drive. Yes, 50 main characters with their own struggles, not NPCs. Five per minute.

The People Who Never Age

Have you noticed how some people seem frozen at a specific age in your mind?

The person who runs the corner store near your house. How old are they? You've been going there for years, but if someone asked you if they're 35 or 55, you honestly couldn't say. They're just... corner-store people.

The lawyer you see once a year. The gardener who comes every two weeks. The person at the dry cleaners. They exist at whatever age they were when you first encountered them, and they stay that age in your perception even though years pass.

That's NPC thinking. They don't age because they're not actual characters with continuing stories. They're functions. Roles. The person who does the thing you need done.

You don't think about them having birthdays. Getting older. Dealing with back pain preventing them to lift heavy things now. They're static. Part of the scenery.

It's not your fault. It's natural. This pattern shows up everywhere. Teachers should care for students, not just handle them. Managers should care for their teams, not just manage them. CEOs should care for their people, not just lead them.

But when you see people as NPCs, you don't care for them. You handle them. Manage them. Use them for the function they serve in your story. Some people do this on purpose (yeah, that's sad), but most of us do it unconsciously.

The Social Media Feed of NPCs

Someone posts about their father passing away. Within minutes, someone comments: "Yes, I remember MY father. He was so special to me."

Someone shares their engagement news. The comments fill with: "This makes ME so happy! I'm so happy for you guys..."

Their moment. Their announcement. Their pain. Their joy.

And within seconds, someone has made it about themselves.

It's comment hijacking. Taking someone else's story and using it as a stage to perform your own narrative.

Someone gets a promotion at work. Instead of celebrating, someone else immediately responds: "Must be nice. I've been here longer and never got promoted."

The promoted colleague's achievement became her coworker's rant.

Someone shares something they're proud of, a meal they cooked, a project they finished, a milestone they reached. Someone has to comment: "I did that years ago. It was delicious!"

One person's moment became another's comparison point.

The person posting wasn't asking for parallel stories. They weren't looking for someone else's experience. They were sharing THEIR moment.

But to the commenter, that post is just content. Just another NPC dialogue box that appeared in their feed. And dialogue boxes exist to give you something to respond to, right? To give you a quest, to trigger your own story.

Because in a feed full of NPCs, their stories don't matter as stories. They matter as content. As opportunities. As a stage for your performance.

When everyone else is just a character in your game, their moments exist to serve your narrative. Their struggles exist to showcase how you've struggled more. Their joys exist to remind everyone of your joys.

The feed reinforces the NPC thinking more than any other space. Because you're not looking at people. You're scrolling through content. And content exists for you to consume, react to, and make about yourself. At the end of the day, it's your feed, right?

They're not people sharing their lives. They're characters delivering dialogue that you can respond to however you want.

Until something reminds you they're not.

The Uber Driver in Mexico City

I was in Mexico City on a Friday evening. Payroll Friday. If you know Mexico City, you know what that means. The entire city becomes a parking lot. Everyone's got money, everyone's going somewhere, and every street is gridlocked.

I needed to get to the airport. I was heading home after a work trip, and timing was tight. The Uber app showed the route—the shortest one in terms of minutes, but in Mexico City traffic, if you miss one turn, the entire trip can add 20-30 minutes because you can't just circle back. You're stuck in the chaos.

First, the driver was late in picking me up.

Then during the ride, he missed one significant turn.

I watched the ETA jump from 45 minutes to 60 minutes. I was now recalculating arrivals, gate times, security lines. In my subconscious, the driver wasn't executing his function properly. He was a service person who was supposed to get me there efficiently, and he wasn't doing that.

Then his phone rang.

I heard his wife's voice through the speaker. Then he answered: "Sorry, honey. I'm stuck in traffic with a client. I'll be there as soon as I can."

Her response: "Take care, baby. God bless you."

That's it.

He wasn't just a driver who missed a turn anymore. He was a person dealing with the same chaos I was dealing with. With a wife who understood that Friday payroll traffic is impossible. Who called him "baby", who said "God bless you" with patience instead of frustration.

From the car smell, I could tell that he smoked, so to clear the air (pun intended), I offered him a cigarette in the middle of the chaos. He felt relieved. Told me he'd been out of cigarettes and had been craving one since his lunch break. We did some chitchat to fill the silence, nothing deep in particular. But we both felt kind of relieved. I wasn't that late to my flight—the added delay just cut short my reading time at the gate.

I'm not saying that phone call changed my life or woke me up to some profound truth. I'm saying it reminded me of something I already knew but kept forgetting: this person has a complete life. He's not just executing a function in my story. He has someone at home who cares about him. He has his own version of the stress I'm feeling. For him, I was an NPC that evening. I was his decision (accepting my ride request on his app) that ended up delaying his arriving early to his wife at home.

That's what I mean about NPCs. We know intellectually that everyone is a person. But we forget it constantly. Especially when they're not performing the way we need them to perform in our story.

Everyone in This Traffic

Look around you right now. You're on the highway, in traffic. How many cars can you see?

Ten? Fifty?

Every single one has a person inside. A full person with a complete life.

The person on the bus isn't just taking up space on the road. They're heading somewhere that matters to them—work, home, an appointment, someone they care about.

The person walking on the sidewalk isn't just a pedestrian you need to watch for. They're dealing with something. Maybe they're worried about money. Maybe they're excited about a date tonight. Maybe they just got news that changed everything.

The teenager with the college jacket three cars ahead isn't just a slow driver learning to navigate traffic. They're stressed about the midterm exam. Trying to figure out how to fit in. Wondering if anyone noticed them today. Carrying the weight of being a teenager in a world that demands they know what they want to be before they even know who they are.

Everyone you see is struggling with something. Everyone is trying to figure something out. Everyone has people depending on them and people they depend on.

We need teachers who see their students as humans, not just names on a roster. Managers who see their teams as people, not just resources. CEOs who see their employees as individuals with lives, not just functions on an organization chart.

That's what it means to stop seeing NPCs and start seeing people.

The Magic Lens That Shows Their Stories

Imagine for a second that you're wearing augmented reality glasses. But these are special—they have the unique feature that when you looked at any person, you saw a movie poster floating above their head —the poster for their all-time favorite film.

You're walking through the mall. Above one person's head: *The Shawshank Redemption*. Another: *Star Wars*. Someone else: *The Godfather*. That kid over there: *KPop Demon Hunters*.

Now imagine you see someone with YOUR favorite movie above their head.

What would you do?

You'd probably smile. Maybe even approach them. "No way, that's my favorite too!" Suddenly you have something to talk about. A connection. A reason to see them as a real person instead of just another shopper in your way.

You need at least one thing in common to form a community—something shared that makes you both members of the same invisible group. These magic lenses are now community generators.

Take the movie *Moneyball*, for example. If I saw someone with a *Moneyball* poster floating above their head, I'd want to talk to them immediately. Because that movie tells me something about them. They appreciate analytics. They love baseball. They're drawn to stories about disruption and going against conventional wisdom. They probably enjoyed Brad Pitt and Jonah Hill's chemistry. That one movie reveals entire dimensions of who they are (yes, this is my favorite movie, and that's why I dedicated 8 sentences to it where 3 could've done the trick).

Every person has special interests and fears and dreams and memories. Things that make them laugh. Things that keep them up at night. Stories they tell themselves about who they are.

But you can't see any of that when you're in traffic. You just see a car. An obstacle. An NPC blocking your lane.

The person in front of you going exactly the speed limit? Maybe they just got their license back after losing it. Maybe they have a baby sleeping in the backseat. Maybe they're driving their elderly parent to a doctor's appointment, and they're scared of any sudden movements.

The "aggressive" driver weaving through lanes? Maybe they just got a call that their kid is in the emergency room. Maybe they're about to miss their flight. Maybe they're just aggressive drivers—but even that is because of something in their story, some combination of experiences and pressures that makes them drive that way.

You don't have magic augmented reality glasses. You can't see their favorite movies or their internal worlds.

But now you can remember they're there. And once you do, it opens up all kinds of interesting possibilities.

Escaping the NPC Mindset

The person at the gym kicking people out of their camera shot? They were seeing NPCs.

Those stadium fights we talked about. Two people risking everything, seeing each other as opposing fighters. NPCs to defeat.

People on tight schedules at Disney, rushing from ride to ride. They were NPCs during your visit for you to feel relaxed because they looked stressed.

Stupid people you want to move ahead of in line. NPCs programmed to frustrate you.

The car that cut you off without signaling. An NPC with bad programming.

The person who took your parking spot. An NPC stealing your resources.

Every example was of someone forgetting that other people aren't NPCs.

The Uber driver in Mexico City traffic reminded me of that on the spot. Not because I became enlightened, but because I got a glimpse behind the NPC and saw the person taking that phone call.

And once you see it, you can't fully unsee it.

You'll forget. You'll slip back into NPC mode. You'll get frustrated at the slow driver. You'll get annoyed at the late service worker and forget they had three other clients before you.

That's normal. That's human.

There's no exam for holding everyone's full humanity in your head at all times. That's impossible. 30,000 people at a concert? You can't see all their lives simultaneously. You can't realize all of their individual plans they needed to complete in order to attend that concert. That half of them traveled from another city to be there—planes, hotels, transport, everything. Spent life-savings. Received the trip as a graduation gift. You can't hold the awareness that every single person in that arena has their own hopes and fears and people waiting for them.

There's no exam for how quickly you catch yourself slipping back into NPC mode either. You will slip. You'll forget. You'll treat someone as scenery or an obstacle or a function.

And then something will remind you. A moment of eye contact. A realization that hits you in the middle of traffic chaos.

Not NPCs but co-characters in their own stories, driving alongside yours on the same highway.

That's the shift. Not perfection. Just awareness that you can return to when you remember.

And sometimes, that's enough to turn a frustrating delay into a shared cigarette in the middle of chaos.

Chapter 14

THE MERGE YOU GIVE

So once you see people as people instead of NPCs, what do you do with that awareness?

Recognition alone doesn't change much. You're stuck in this rush hour traffic with everyone else. Someone's trying to merge from a gas station entrance a few cars ahead. They're clearly stuck, the nose of their car inching forward every time there's a gap, but nobody's letting them in.

You can acknowledge that the person has their own full life, their own reasons for being here, their own stress about being late—and still refuse to let them merge because you have the right of way. "Hum!"

Recognition without action changes nothing.

The Japanese have a word for the next step—*omoiyari*. It's deeper than empathy. It's anticipating someone's needs without them having to say anything. Responding with quiet, thoughtful care. Small, unspoken kindnesses that show you're not just aware other people exist, but that you're actively making space for them.

Not grand gestures. Not performative kindness for social media. Just the subtle acts that show deep respect and sensitivity to others.

Understanding Empathy and Sympathy

Some people use these words interchangeably. They're not the same thing, and the difference matters when we talk about *omoiyari*.

Sympathy is an emotional response: "Oh, that's so sad. I'm sorry for you." It's feeling bad about someone's situation. It validates their pain, makes them feel heard, but doesn't necessarily lead anywhere.

Empathy is understanding: "Why did that happen? Can it be fixed?" It's putting yourself in their position deeply enough to see potential solutions. It cares enough to want to change the situation, not just acknowledge it.

When someone tells you they're struggling, sympathy says, "That must be hard." Empathy says, "What would help right now?"

One offers comfort. The other offers to address the cause.

Both have their place—sometimes people genuinely just need to be heard and validated. But if someone's car breaks down on the side of the road, "I'm so sorry that happened to you" doesn't get them moving again. "Do you need jumper cables or a ride?" does.

People sometimes need to feel comforted before considering solutions. That's valid.

Omoiyari leans toward empathy—anticipates needs and acts on them. It's empathy in motion. Empathy that doesn't wait to be asked.

You could keep going past that merging car. You have the right of way. You're already late.

Or you could stop. Create space. Wave them in. It's not weakness. It's the smart move.

Takes you three seconds longer. Changes their entire next five minutes.

That's *omoiyari*. Not because you're a saint, but because you remember what it felt like to be stuck, watching everyone pretend they don't see you.

Someone let you in once. So you let someone else in. Not expecting gratitude. Just making space.

Think about parking lots. When you get a new car, you park away from everyone else—protecting your doors from dings. That's self-preservation.

But there's another version: parking away so the person next to you has room to open their door without worrying. Same behavior, different motivation. One is about protecting yourself. The other is about making space for someone else.

That's *omoiyari* in a parking spot.

The Third Burger in Rome

One time my wife and I were vacationing in Rome to celebrate our anniversary. I remember one day that we were very tired to go out for lunch. We were staying at the IQ Hotel, and there was a McDonald's on the corner of Via Firenze and Via Nazionale (I later found out they moved it one street ahead), just three blocks away from the hotel. So I suggested to her that maybe I could just walk out to get us some food.

Not to brag, but my Italian was pretty good for most of the trip—I'd studied intensely for like two months before we left. At a bus stop, I even got to give directions in Italian to a tourist from Palermo who was visiting *la città,* straight out from Sicily; my wife couldn't believe the scene (neither could I, because he *did* understand me).

So, when I went into the restaurant, I placed my order confidently. After I paid and walked out the door, I realized I had three burgers in my bag. I'd messed up—my flawed Italian had me ordering three burgers instead of two. I smiled. Now I had a fun story to tell her back at the hotel about my "confident" Italian.

But when I stepped out, there was a homeless guy sitting outside with his dog.

I handed him the third burger.

Didn't make it a moment. Didn't film it. Didn't post about it. Just handed it to him. He thanked me. I nodded and started walking.

Then I looked back.

He was sharing half of it with his dog.

Honest truth about this? That felt really, really awesome. And I loved that feeling. That feeling was for me—no video, no cameras, no validation from anyone else—it was mine.

(Watching him share it with his dog, for me as a dog person, was the cherry on top.)

That's the way I want to live. Having those feelings.

Maybe that is labeled selfish from your passenger seat. But for me, is an amazing feeling that now I always try to replicate whenever possible. As one dear cousin says, "if the family economy allows it."

Because that's what *omoiyari* becomes in practice. Not the grand gesture. Not the documented act of charity. Just buying an extra burger and handing it to someone who needs it more than you do. Most of the time there's even a low-cost add-on promo at the counter to make it easier.

I'm not saying this to show off or to get praise. I'm writing these down to invite you to do the same. These slight gestures make our community better. For example, I keep water bottles in my car now like the old Uber. Two or three new ones. At traffic light stops, when someone reaches out asking for money or even to wipe my windshield —or just vendors selling stuff at the traffic light—instead of or on top of giving them some change, I hand out a water bottle. Especially on sunny days.

They love the water bottle.

My wife nowadays pushes me to do this at home too, with every food or package delivery. Especially those on motorcycles, sweating inside their helmets. There's always a 500ml bottle of water in the fridge for them.

You see a homeless person outside the convenience store? Maybe buying an extra soda on your way out and handing it over would make their day more than dropping loose change in their cup.

Small things. But they add up.

Choosing When You Have Capacity

Once you pay attention to other people's unexpressed needs, you can't stop noticing them.

The person struggling with the heavy door. The family trying to figure out the subway map. The elderly man who can't reach the item on the top shelf.

And you have to choose. Because you can't help everyone every time.

Which means sometimes you'll see someone who needs help and you'll keep walking because you're at your limit and you can't take on one more thing.

And that's okay.

There's no exam for being endlessly available to everyone. *Omoiyari* doesn't mean sacrificing yourself constantly.

It means paying attention when you have the capacity. Acting when you can. Creating space when it costs you nothing or something manageable.

Sometimes the most empathetic thing you can do is recognize you're depleted and need to preserve your energy for the people in your immediate life who depend on you.

The key is being honest with yourself: am I actually at capacity, or am I just not wanting to be inconvenienced?

There's a difference between "I genuinely don't have bandwidth" and "I don't feel like it."

One is self-preservation. The other is just selfishness.

And sometimes you won't know which one it is until later. That's fine too. You will not get this right every time.

The Thing About Small Gestures

Omoiyari isn't about big demonstrations of kindness. It's not about making yourself the hero of someone else's story.

It's about the tiny adjustments you make because you're paying attention.

Holding the door for someone carrying boxes—but not making them hurry because you're holding it.

Moving your bag from the empty seat when the train fills up—before anyone has to ask.

Lowering your music when you notice someone nearby trying to concentrate.

Offering the aisle seat to someone taller when you're on an airplane and you're short enough that leg room doesn't matter as much to you.

Asking your colleague if they need anything from the coffee shop when you're already going—not because you're trying to be nice, but because you're going anyway and carrying two drinks instead of one costs you nothing.

These moments don't earn you points. Nobody's keeping score. There's no exam for how often you anticipate others' needs.

But they change the texture of daily life. For you and for them.

You are now constantly aware of the people around you.

Everyone around you.

Everyone.

I mean, every person you see... since the minute you woke up.

(Did you get the hint?)

Yes, at home.

Here is the main point of the chapter: your partner is also not an NPC.

They're not there to fulfill the role of your partner. They have a life, desires, goals, dreams—not for you, but theirs. And sometimes, if you're lucky, those dreams are WITH you in the picture.

Omoiyari with your partner looks like: ordering their favorite beverage without them asking. Changing the toilet paper before it runs out—not leaving them with the last pieces so they're the ones stuck changing it. Refilling their water bottle when you see it's empty. Charging their phone when you notice it has low battery. Moving their car keys to where they can see them when you know they're running late.

Small anticipations that show, "I'm paying attention to your life, not just mine."

That's *omoiyari*.

Or as Dean Martin would say, "that's *amore*."

Not waiting for them to ask for help. Not keeping score. There's no exam of who does that more than the other. Just noticing when they're overwhelmed and acting on it before they have to request support.

That's what makes relationships feel like partnerships instead of negotiations.

If you're not in a relationship, look towards your parents. They aren't here just to provide for you (cue the *cliché* ATM reference).

Omoiyari with your parents looks like: taking them out to dinner, your treat, just because. Calling them to share something funny that happened, not just when you need something. Showing up to help with the thing they've been putting off, without waiting for them to ask.

Small acts that say, "I remember you exist as people, not just as the people who raised me." They are people. They also have a bucket list.

Have you asked them about their list? Is there something on it you could facilitate without being asked to?

If they are still around, you should share more with them. And not just the debt on your credit card.

Anticipating Before Being Asked

You're checking your rearview mirror. You see a car behind you coming up rapidly. You don't wait for them to flash their headlights like it's an ambulance siren. You just change lanes before they have to signal, because you're aware someone's in a rush and you can anticipate.

Driving on the highway and you suddenly encounter a traffic jam. You turn on your hazard lights as a precaution. There's no traffic rule requiring this, but you're thinking about the person behind you who maybe hasn't noticed that traffic ahead is stopped. Sure, it's also for your own security, but that's *omoiyari* too—anticipating what someone else might need to know before they realize they need it.

Small moments of creating space without announcement.

And gradually, your commute changes. Not because traffic gets better, but because you're actively taking part in making it slightly less adversarial for everyone involved.

Not racing anymore. Not competing. Just coexisting. Anticipating. Making space.

That's what you do with the awareness that other people aren't NPCs.

You drive as if they matter. Because they do.

And there's no exam for how often you remember this. You'll forget sometimes. You'll be stressed and snap at someone who didn't deserve it. You'll be in a hurry and not create space when you could have.

That's normal.

But the times you remember? Those moments when you pause and create space and someone's day gets slightly easier because you were paying attention?

Those add up.

Not on any official scorecard. Not toward any grade.

Just miles on everyone's odometer. Including yours.

And sometimes that quiet act of anticipating someone's need without them having to ask becomes the moment they remember years later when they think about their commute.

The person who let them merge. The stranger who held the door. The moment someone saw them struggling, and helped without making it a production.

You might not remember doing it.

But they'll remember someone did.

And maybe next time, they'll create space for someone else.

Not because they're trying to pay it forward or balance some cosmic ledger.

Just because they remember what it felt like to have someone anticipate their needs and respond with quiet, thoughtful care. Friendship is everything when you're on a long drive.

That's *omoiyari*.

That's the art of seeing others.

And it's what makes the highway feel a little less like a competition and a little more like a shared journey, even when we are all stuck in this traffic jam.

Chapter 15

STOP SIGNS EXIST FOR A REASON

O kay, there's no exam. There's no grading system. There's no competition you need to win. There's no judge evaluating your route against everyone else's.

But there ARE rules. Rules are good. Welcome to the real world— it has rules, and ignoring them doesn't make them disappear.

Before you think I just contradicted the entire book premise, let me explain. Traffic laws exist. Red lights. Speed limits. Stop signs. Lane markers. These aren't there to grade your performance or rank you against other drivers. They're there so we don't crash into each other.

You can take any route you want. You can go at your own speed. You can change lanes when you need to. But you can't run red lights and plow through intersections because "there's no exam." That's not freedom—that's chaos.

The Entitlement

Some people say the entitlement, especially on social media, is generational. But this isn't a specific age trait. We are all doing this, subconsciously or not. Everyone is the main character of their own story (which we are). But some people can't handle when someone else's story takes center stage for five minutes. If they're the protagonist, you're supposed to be background. When you post about YOUR life, they feel like they've been demoted to supporting characters.

So they hijack the moment. They redirect attention. They make your post about them. And here's the thing: they don't know we know. They don't realize we can see through the redirect.

You're absolutely entitled to live your life. Post your breakfast. Share your wins. Celebrate your milestones. But you're not entitled to shove your life into someone else's moment and demand equal attention.

If someone's celebrating, let them celebrate. If someone's grieving, let them grieve. If someone's sharing joy, don't respond with your resume of superior joy. Unwritten rules.

Not because there's an exam on being supportive, but because there ARE people on this highway, and they have rights to their moments just like you have rights to yours.

The Unwritten Rules

Someone's sports team wins? Let them enjoy it. Don't immediately pivot to, "Well, MY team won more championships." Their moment isn't about you.

Someone gets a raise at work? Celebrate it. Don't think, "Why them, not me?" They're not taking that raise out of your salary. Their success didn't subtract from your paycheck. "Let" them have it.

Someone shares something they're proud of? Let them be proud. You don't need to one-up. You don't need to critique. You don't need to make it about you. There is no exam on who is prouder.

> "The only occasion to justify looking down on someone is while you are helping them up."
>
> — NEIL DEGRASSE TYSON, *STARRY MESSENGER*,
>
> 149.

This applies to undermining other people's moments. The size of your achievements is only relative to you, not to them. Your emotions are only relative to you, not to them. You don't have to diminish someone else's actions just because you think yours are better. You are not superior to them in emotions or possessions.

Not because you're being graded on kindness (you're not), but because you're sharing the highway with other humans who are also the center of their own lives. And their lives deserves the same respect you expect for yours. Their choices. Their moments. Even their freedom:

The Cecilia Giménez Lesson

Years ago, you may have heard about this one. An art curator named Cecilia Giménez attempted to restore the painting *Ecce Homo* in her local church. It went wrong. Very wrong. The internet exploded. Memes everywhere.

But then something darker happened: people demanded she face criminal charges. They wanted her prosecuted. Some wanted her locked up.

Prison.

Over a bad restoration of a painting.

Think about that. People who claimed to love art, who posted endlessly about the importance of preserving culture and respecting history, were willing to destroy a human being's freedom over a painting.

I understand that art has value. I understand cultural preservation matters. But the desire to punish someone's life, to value a painting over her freedom, felt insane to me.

It made me think about what we actually value when we say we value art:

If you saw at the Louvre a perfect copy of the *Mona Lisa*, indistinguishable from the original, you wouldn't "feel the same" knowing it was a replica. Why? I mean, the visual experience is identical. The technique, the composition, the colors—all are there.

We value the fact that a human made it. That Leonardo da Vinci's actual hands touched that canvas centuries ago.

Today, with generative artificial intelligence, you can create magnificent art in every style. Technically flawless. Aesthetically stunning. But we don't praise it the same way, obviously, because an AI model generated it.

I'm starting to truly believe that we don't actually appreciate the art pieces themselves. We definitely appreciate humans capable of creating art with their hands, but not the end piece itself.

So when people demanded Cecilia face prison time, they revealed something: their attachment to the painting that most didn't know about a week before, mattered more than her humanity. She became an NPC in their story about protecting art. A villain to punish. A symbol used to make an example of.

She was 81 years old when the incident happened. She volunteered her time to help her church. She didn't profit. She vandalized nothing. She just... failed at something she attempted in good faith.

The Three Cars Practice

Here's something practical you will do starting today.

During your day: let three cars merge ahead of you.

Not two. Not five. Three.

Why three specifically? There's a psychology behind this. When stores sell eggs by the dozen, people learn to buy twelve. Not eleven. Not thirteen. The number becomes the standard. It's called the anchoring effect in marketing. The first number you encounter becomes your reference point.

The nudge theory shows us that small, specific prompts change behavior more effectively than vague suggestions. "Be kind" doesn't stick. "Let three cars merge" does.

And there's the scarcity principle at work too. Three feels manageable, not endless. It's enough to be intentional but not so many that it feels like a burden you'll quit doing after a week.

Three cars during your entire commute. Three small gestures

during your day. Three moments where you create space for someone else.

Not because there's an exam on daily kindness. But because the practice changes something in you.

When you let the three cars merge, you're not just helping them, you're reminding yourself they're not an NPC. They have somewhere to be. They're stressed about being late. They needed the gap you just created.

This isn't just for them. It's for you. It's the awareness practice that keeps you from slipping back into NPC thinking, where everyone around you is just scenery in your commute.

Three. Not four. Not seven.

Not because it's a magic number, but because it's specific enough to remember and small enough to actually do.

Some days you'll forget and do only one. But when you remember, when you consciously create space three times during your day, that's when the highway stops feeling like a competition and starts feeling like we are all a community of people trying to get somewhere. And I'll be there for you, because you're there for me too.

Three cars. Three gestures. Three moments of recognizing someone else's route matter as much as yours.

Start today.

The Harsh Oxymoron

"I care enough about you that I don't care about your daily life."

That even sounded mean, right? It's quite the opposite.

Happiness isn't caring about feeling superior to others or making them feel less than you. It's not relative. Happiness is living your life with no need to measure it against everyone else's dashboard.

I care enough about you to want you to live well. I care enough to respect your route. I care enough to let you make your own choices and celebrate your own wins.

But I don't need and I don't want to monitor your life. I don't need to compete with your achievements. I don't need your validation of my route or your permission to take mine.

It's not indifference. It's respect.

The Ant Colony

Ants follow rules. Not because there's an ant police grading their performance, but because the colony only survives when everyone respects the system.

No ant demands the best food. No ant hijacks another ant's path to make it about them. No ant refuses to contribute because of "what's in it for me?" They don't sacrifice themselves for recognition or praise. They just follow the collective rules that keep the colony functioning.

We're smarter than ants. We can question. We can ask, "Why should I follow these rules?" We can calculate whether respecting someone else's moment serves our interests. We can decide that our need for attention is more important than someone else's right to their achievement.

But maybe that's not the flex we think it is.

If we're sharing this highway, this traffic jam, if we're living on this planet together, we not only need, we want to follow our rules. Not because there's an exam on following them, but because without them, we're just millions of individuals crashing into each other constantly. Rules help control the fun.

The ants figured this out. We should too.

The Rules Aren't Grading You

Traffic laws don't judge your route. They just make sure you don't crash into someone while you're taking it.

Same with these rules about respecting others. They're not measuring your performance as a human. They're not ranking you on a kindness leaderboard. I know—it feels unfair. But red lights don't care about your schedule. They're just saying: your route is yours, their route is theirs, and both can exist without collision if you respect the space between you.

You don't need to be perfect at this. You're allowed your road rage.

You're allowed your frustration when someone cuts you off. You're allowed not to always be in the mood to let people merge.

But when you get too clever and try to jump the line, then ask the car in front for permission to cut in and enter the highway, when you make someone's moment about you, when you're demanding attention as a right instead of earning it through genuine connection, when you're treating people like NPCs in your story instead of protagonists in theirs, those aren't violations of an exam, those are violations of the unwritten rules we're discussing here that let us all share this highway without constant collision.

The Gestalt Prayer

Fritz Perls, the founder of Gestalt therapy, wrote a statement that should probably be printed on highway signs:

> I do my thing and you do your thing.
> I am not in this world to live up to your expectations,
> And you are not in this world to live up to mine.
> You are you, and I am I.
> If by chance we find each other, it's beautiful.
> If not, it can't be helped.
> I lack love for myself
> when, in trying to please you, I betray myself.
> I lack love for you
> when I try to make you be as I want you to be
> instead of accepting you as you truly are.
> You are you, and I am me.
>
> — FRITZ PERLS

That's it. That's the entire philosophy in twelve lines.

You take your route. I take mine. If our paths cross and we travel together for a while, amazing. If not, that's okay too.

But while we're sharing the highway? We follow the rules. We respect each other's spaces. We let people have their moments. We don't run red lights and assume everyone else will accommodate us.

There's no judge watching to see if you're good enough.

But there ARE people. And they're not decorations on your route. They're on their own routes, and those routes are just as real as yours.

Respect the rules. Not because you'll be graded on it, but because that's how we all get where we're going without destroying each other along the way.

Part Six

THE OPEN ROAD

Highway opens up, driving at your own speed.

Chapter 16

TODAY IS 100% OF YOUR COMMUTE

During my 45th birthday, I remember feeling genuinely proud. Not because I'd achieved some checklist or hit some milestone. But because I thought, in an optimistic manner, that I was at the peak of my lifespan. The middle. Halfway through.

I'd ask myself: "Do I feel old?" Hell no. I'm only halfway through my life. Hoping for 90 years, right? That felt good. That felt like control.

Then I started noticing something.

People around me were dying at what everyone calls "young age." Tragic accidents. Celebrities. Athletes. Pandemic. People I admired.

Paul Walker. I enjoy the Fast and Furious franchise a lot. And he died in a tragic car accident. Just like that.

Kobe Bryant. Died on a standard commute. Not even in an extreme helicopter stunt. Just going somewhere with his daughter.

Matthew Perry. Iconic character from Friends. Chandler, the tv king of sarcasm. Overdose.

Countless friends and close family members during COVID.

And realizing: that's it. That was their whole life.

Not halfway. Not "still had 30 years left." That was 100% of what they got.

Then I read an article about a technique of counting down your summers, literally, to make the most out of the ones you got left: "How Many Summers Do You Have Left?" Take your age, subtract from 80 or 90, and that's your remaining summers. Better make them count!

My immediate reaction? I hated it.

Not only I hate living under pressure. That's not living at all.

This is what happens if you live by countdown: you go on a trip and if something goes wrong—if you get a flat tire and don't arrive at your destination—that moment becomes miserable. You "missed" your window. Now you have to rearrange everything, or live with the guilt that this experience "didn't count."

(But I can see clearly now. That also counted. You've got a flat tire. You met people in the nearest town who helped you. You saw how their life is slower than yours. How their minds are just thinking about next Sunday because that's when there's "The Dance" at the public kiosk in the middle of town.)

That's also living. Discovering new experiences. But if you're racing against a countdown, you miss it entirely. You're too busy being angry about the delay.

Pressure of having 15 summers left? 30 summers left? No, I hated that approach.

So, I started wondering. Reflecting. Trying to debunk it: wait a minute, why are you so sure you'll live to 85?

"Because that's the stat."

You looked at the numbers, but you didn't really look. Stats are just an explanation of what has happened. That's why statistics and probability are close but not the same. Stats tell you what occurred in the past, performance. They don't predict YOUR specific future.

How naïve we are to put ourselves in the same bag as a statistic based on random people—people who only died from natural causes, because accidents are outliers to the statistic—people who lived completely different routes than ours?

That's when I started trying to see it the other way around.

The Countdown Fallacy

Remember? You are the standard. Your life, your pace, your route.

But that "80 years" or "90 years" average? It comes from millions of people who lived completely different routes than yours. Different genetics. Different habits. Different vehicles. Different highways entirely.

Some of us are constantly on the interstate—high-speed, high-stress, burning through fuel. Some of us are on a wagon going up from the farm to our house in the woods—slow and steady, minimal wear.

We drive very different cars at very different paces.

You're not an ant. We're not a species that behaves almost identically, where you could reasonably predict everyone's lifespan based on the colony average—with some tiny margin of error.

Your route is yours. Your vehicle is yours. Your pace is yours.

Counting down "25 summers left" based on someone else's odometer reading makes no sense. You don't know how many summers you have. Nobody does. You might have 50. You might have 5. You might have 1.

But what you DO have is this summer. Right now. And when next summer comes, you'll have that one too.

Behind Schedule

I was 32 years old when I asked Silvana to be my girlfriend. October 25th, 2009. We got engaged exactly one year later—same date. Married on October 22nd, 2011.

Before Silvana, I had two girlfriends. The first one lasted about three weeks when I was 17. The second one lasted a month and a half when I was 20.

That means I spent 12 years "without a girlfriend." And in my hometown, where everyone marries around 25, I was way late in life. I was behind schedule.

One friend told me—as justification for why he was getting married in his 20s—"You need to marry in your 20s so you can play with your kids in your 30s." He was so confident that was the correct way, because in your 40s, you can't run anymore the way you can in your 30s.

According to what timeline? According to whose route? Why would I not be able to play with my kid in my 40s?

I didn't marry in my 20s. I married at 34. And you know what? I still get to play with my son. The timeline my friend imposed—the one that made me feel behind—was completely arbitrary. It worked on his route. It had nothing to do with mine.

That's the trap of measuring your odometer against someone else's journey.

I've Been Doing This My Whole Life

Think about how that phrase works.

When you're 15 years old and you say, "I've been skateboarding my whole life," you mean 15 years. That's the complete span of your existence, and skateboarding has been part of it the entire time. The 100% of your whole life.

When you're 40 years old and you say, "I've been working in tech my whole life," you mean 40 years (or however long your career has been, your 25 effective working years). That's your 100% professional journey.

Your odometer shows the complete distance you've traveled. All of it. That's not a fraction of some predicted total—that's the whole thing. Your whole life, right there on the dashboard. It doesn't read 15,000 out of 90,000 miles.

At 15, your whole life was 15 years. At 26, your whole life is 26 years. At 48, your whole life is 48 years. That's 100%. Not 60% waiting for the remaining 40%. Not halfway to some imaginary finish line. 100%.

The 100% Reset

Here's where it gets interesting.

Most people think about life like a battery draining. You start at 100%, and every year that passes, you lose a percentage. By 50, you're at "half" your life. At 75, you're on the "last stretch."

But that's not how your odometer works.

Your odometer doesn't count down. It counts up.

Every mile you drive gets added to your total. Every year you live becomes part of your complete journey. You're not losing life—you're accumulating it.

At 26 years old, your life isn't "26 out of a possible 80." Your life IS 26 years. That's 100% of what you've lived. That's the complete measure of your existence so far.

When you turn 27, you don't become "27 out of 80." You become 27 years old—your new 100%. Your reference resets. Your complete life is now one year longer.

This isn't semantics. This changes how you experience time.

When you count down ("I have 25 summers left"), every summer that passes feels like a loss. You're burning through a limited resource. The countdown creates anxiety, urgency, pressure. You're racing against a clock that might not even apply to you.

When you count up ("This is summer number 48 for me"), every summer that arrives is a gift. You didn't lose anything—you gained a new one. And when the next summer comes, it becomes part of your new 100%.

You get one extra summer every year. And once you've experienced it, it becomes part of your completed 100%—not a deduction from some arbitrary total, but an addition to your actual life.

Perspective: Every Morning You Wake Up

Every time you wake up, you are blessed. You are here, and you can take a new drive.

There are people in the trenches right now only hoping to make it to the next day. There are homeless people hoping to make it through the day without starving. There are people in oppressive or war-torn countries hoping to make it to tomorrow, or just trying to enjoy the moment because a sudden attack could happen any minute now.

This is not me being catastrophic. This is the reality for millions of people.

Ask them if they feel like they're halfway through their timeline.

Your ability to even think about tomorrow—to plan ahead, to aim for something beyond today—is already a privilege. So if you want to think about the future, here's a better framework than counting down summers you might not have.

The 5% Aim

You're at your 100% right now. But let's say you want to think about the future. Let's say you want to aim for something beyond today.

Instead of counting down from an arbitrary number, aim for an extra 5% beyond your current 100%.

Not 20%. Not 30%.

How far will you go? Just 5%.

You're 40 years old? Your 100% is 40 years. Aim for an extra 5%—that's 2 more years to stay healthy, take care of yourself, make choices that support your body and mind. You can envision how you want to spend the next 2 years of your work life. That extra 5% is very reasonable. You can handle that. You already know how to live—you've done it for 40 years. Adding just 5% more seems doable.

Here's the beauty of the 5% framework: the older you get, the bigger that 5% becomes in absolute terms, but the more equipped you are to handle it. The percentage is relative to your age.

5% of 20 years is 1 year. 5% of 60 years is 3 years. 5% of 90 years is 4.5 years.

The number grows, but so does your competence. Your wisdom. You've spent your entire life learning how to take care of yourself, how to navigate your route, how to manage your vehicle. Every extra year makes you better at it.

And when you hit that extra 5%, it doesn't stays "5% extra." It becomes part of your new 100%.

If you're 40 and you aimed for 42, when you reach 42, that's not "105% of your predicted life." That's your new 100%. Your complete life. Your full odometer reading.

You can make it 10% instead of 5%. The principle is the same. The point is this: you're not chasing some external timeline. You're building on what you've already accomplished. And every day you live becomes part of your completed 100%, not a percentage deducted from some imaginary total.

Future-You Owns Future 100%

Here's the part that's tricky to explain, but crucial to understand:

You don't have "unaccomplished things" sitting on today's 100%.

Your life right now—your 100%—is complete. It's not missing anything. You haven't failed at things you "should have done by now" because this 100% is what you've actually done, not what you think you should have done.

Your 100% is what has defined you as a person.

That's what you are. You are not the plans in your future that haven't occurred yet.

Future-you will own your future 100%. Not current-you.

If there's something you want to do, something you want to experience, something you want to accomplish—that belongs on future-you's odometer. When you get there, it'll become part of that 100%. But it's not absent from your this 100%, because your current 100% is complete as it is.

You don't have ideas for the future. Those ideas are here in your present—you already have them. You'll have different ideas in the future, but you're not living there yet. Live today. Decide which ideas make sense and do them today, because those are your present ideas. The future ideas belong to future-you.

Stop measuring what you haven't done yet against an imaginary timeline. Stop thinking, "I'm 35 and I should have already [bought a house / had kids / started a business / traveled the world]."

Should have according to whom? According to what timeline? According to which route?

Your route is yours. Your 100% is what you've lived, not what you think you were supposed to live. And when you do those things—if you do those things—they'll become part of your future 100%, which will be just as complete as your current 100%.

What Living at 100% Looks Like

A friend of mine was living in countdown mode. Stressed. Always planning. Always measuring. Always feeling behind.

I shared this perspective with him. The 100% concept. The idea that he's already complete right now.

He told me later that the stress came out of his system. He was living in a future that isn't here yet. He started living today.

Now he allows himself not to do anything on one day if he doesn't want to. There's no quota he has to fulfill. He answers to his current present self.

I've been there too. There was a time I'd wake up at 4am to bid on Air Jordan 1s on eBay. Trying to steal them from other bidders. Well, I'm not a thief. I'm a fan. The point is, I was racing against what? Some imaginary deadline? Like I was running out of time to "complete" a sneaker collection that had no actual finish line. My compulsion had 34 pairs already, but I couldn't see I was already complete. I was counting what I still needed to get instead of what I'd already accumulated. That urgency—that countdown pressure—was creating the stress.

And while I'm writing this book, I can embrace even more that this is my 100%. This isn't just a book for my bucket list. Leaving today this "there's no exam" message written is the most tangible way of transcending years after I'm gone.

I'm fully aware that I am at my 100%. That tomorrow is not a given. And my soul would be disappointed if I hadn't finished this book before I'm gone.

And if someone takes this and revamps it or debunks it and makes it better for society, even then I'm still transcending—because I helped craft what doesn't need to be done.

Yes, that sounds fatalistic. But even my ego wanting to finish this book is aware: we are at our 100% right now.

Look at your odometer right now. How many years does it show? That's not a fraction of some predicted total. That's not "X out of Y." That's your complete journey so far. That's 100% of your life.

They don't sell cars with odometers counting down or with a mileage limit. They always count up the miles.

Every mile behind you is part of your journey. Not preparation for your journey. Not the "setup phase" before your "real life" begins. The miles you've already driven ARE your life.

The years you spent in school? Part of your 100%. The relationships that didn't work out? Part of your 100%. The jobs you tried and left? Part of your 100%. The places you lived? Part of your 100%. The mistakes you made? Part of your 100%. The things you're proud of? Part of your 100%.

All of it. Every single mile. That's your journey. And it's complete.

When you add more miles, you don't complete your journey. You expand it. Your journey was already complete. Now it's complete over a longer distance.

That's the shift.

You're not running out of life. You're accumulating it. You're not halfway to the finish line. You're at 100% of the journey you've lived so far. And tomorrow, you'll be at 100% again, with one more day added.

There is no exam grading whether you've driven far enough yet. There's no scorecard measuring whether your odometer reading is "good" or "behind schedule."

There's just your odometer. Your miles. Your 100%.

And every morning you wake up, that number goes up, not down.

Today is 100% of your life. Tomorrow will be your new 100%. Stop counting down summers you might not have. Start counting up the ones you reach.

Chapter 17

EYES ON THE ROAD

E ven when you're on the right road, heading in the right direction, making progress—your eyes can still be somewhere else.

Glancing at the screen. Checking notifications. Scrolling through someone else's route while you're supposed to be navigating your own.

Literally, while driving. But this is also a reality in every part of our lives.

You can be exactly where you need to be and still miss it entirely. Because being physically present and actually being present aren't the same thing.

The Guardrails That Help

When I get in the car, I open Waze—a navigation app that shows you the route, traffic patterns, and where accidents are happening. It's like Google Maps, with real-time updates from other drivers. I set my destination to get a glimpse of the ETA, and then I place my phone on the dashboard into a magnetic holder that goes in the air vents. The peculiar part of this is that I turn my phone horizontal instead of keeping it vertical.

The reason I started doing this: when the phone's horizontal, you get a broader view of the map. Better panoramic perspective. You can see more of what's coming, especially in the 3D view—it helps you understand the route ahead with more depth.

But I kept doing it for a different reason.

When the phone's horizontal and a text message comes in, the text reply area takes up the entire screen if you try to respond. It's messy. The keyboard blocks everything. Makes texting while driving just inconvenient enough that I won't bother.

I'm creating a guardrail for myself. Not relying on willpower—building a system where the wrong choice becomes harder to make than the right one.

Willpower is finite. It runs out. Especially at the end of a long day when you're tired and stressed and that text notification pings. You might have the discipline to ignore it once, twice, maybe ten times. But eventually, you'll check. Willpower alone isn't enough against the constant pull of distraction.

That's why you need guardrails. Systems that work even when your willpower doesn't.

And when I'm not distracted by trying to text, or checking who just messaged me, or staring at the ETA countdown trying to beat my estimated arrival time, I can actually pay attention to what's happening around me.

Your Road or Someone Else's

But most of the time, we don't build guardrails. We just scroll.

Through other people's vacations. Other people's accomplishments. Other people's carefully curated moments that make their route look better than yours.

You're sitting in your car, driving your route. And you're watching everyone else's highlight reel instead.

Think about your friend's kid. The happiest kid you know, right? Always smiling in photos. Every picture on social media shows them laughing, playing, having the time of their lives.

You see maybe five minutes of their day—the fraction their parents chose to share. And you assume that kid laughs all day. Their life is just pure joy. That your friend has figured out some parenting secret you haven't.

But you don't see the tantrum that happened five minutes before the photo. The meltdown over the wrong-colored cup. The bedtime battle. The moments that don't get posted.

You're watching other people's roads, but you're only seeing the parts they chose to show you. Not even their actual roads. Their edited versions.

And while you're watching their edited roads, you're missing yours.

Maybe you're missing yours on purpose. Maybe you have the tantrums at home, the fight over bedtime, the chaos that doesn't photograph well. And scrolling back to the happiest kid in the world comforts you. Reminds you that other people's lives look easier, better, more put-together than yours feels right now.

The irony is that we're so afraid of missing out on what everyone else is doing that we miss out on what we're actually doing.

You're behind the wheel of your own life, and you're staring at someone else's dashboard.

The Hour That Matters Most

You've probably heard of the ICU at hospitals—intensive care unit. But there's also a place with the acronym NICU. The N stands for Neonatal. Intensive care for newborns.

It's a special place. Rows of incubators. Tiny babies hooked up to monitors and tubes. Nurses who move with such careful precision, like they're handling the most fragile thing in the world. Because they are.

Everyone in that unit has one focus: to help these babies grow, to help them fight, to help them make it.

In 2017, my kids were born prematurely. We spent 78 days in the NICU.

Seventy-eight days of learning a new community—the other parents sharing that space, the doctors, the staff, and especially the nurses. You get to know people in ways you don't expect when you're all in that unit together.

As a parent, you are allowed to spend time at the NICU with your children, but there's a caveat: how much time. It varies by hospital, because the newborns—mostly preemies—can't be exposed to the outside world too much. On average, you're only allowed to visit for one hour per day.

One hour.

That's what you get. An hour to be there, watch them through the incubator, sing to them, tell him about your day, about how you're preparing their room at home. All the things you can't wait to do with them once they're strong enough to leave.

After a preemie reaches their weight and size milestones, after their internal organs develop enough, they get moved to intermediate care. That's when you can finally hold them. Chest-to-chest therapy— skin contact, warmth, heartbeat. The most basic, primal connection between parent and child.

I spent that hour fully immersed. If I could just hold on to that feeling. Watching every tiny movement. Planning the life we were going to have once they came home.

You'd think this is obvious, right? An easy decision to keep your eyes on the road. But it wasn't.

One time I watched a dad in the chair next to me. His baby was on his lap during their chest-to-chest hour. And he was on his phone watching a soccer game.

I remember screaming inside my head: your baby is right there! On your lap. You only get one hour a day. And you're watching a game!?

I'm not judging his parenting overall. I don't know his full story. Our contexts were obviously different. I was a new dad—maybe that was his third child. I struggled with sperm count and motility, and because of that, our pregnancy lasted 5 years, not the standard 9 months. So maybe I was more acutely aware of how precious that hour was.

Maybe he was coping with trauma in the only way he knew how. Maybe watching that game was what kept him from breaking down, from feeling the full weight of having a child in the NICU.

But I am saying this: some moments are irreplaceable.

Some time is worth more than other time.

That one hour with your child in the NICU is worth more than a thousand hours of any game ever played.

Distraction makes everything equal. It treats irreplaceable moments the same as throwaway time.

And once that hour is gone, you can't get it back. You can watch the game on replay. You can catch the highlights. You can see the final score.

That one irreplaceable hour—that's on your road. It may be the most crucial part of your journey so far. And if your eyes aren't on it, you just drove right past the moment that mattered most. You shall not pass it again.

The Documentation Must

The concert you're filming—there's a very strong chance that it's already being captured by professionals with better equipment than you have.

Look around. There's a video crew. Multiple cameras. Professional audio. The wise speak only of what they know—these people know exactly how to capture this moment. That's literally their expertise.

And here you are, holding up your phone, recording a shaky, low-quality version of something that's already being professionally documented by people who actually know what they're doing.

Meanwhile, you're watching the concert through a screen instead of with your eyes. You're so busy making sure you're recording the moment that you're not actually experiencing it.

What if you put your phone down and just watch?

Be present. The video crew capturing the concert—they're looking for crowd energy. They want to show the experience, the excitement, the connection between band and audience. Who do you think they aim their cameras at? The person with a phone blocking their face? Or the person fully immersed, singing along, actually experiencing the moment?

You might even end up being that person in the official footage. The core shot. The "top fan" from the video. And then—this actually happens—the band might reach out to you because you're the famous "top fan" of the band on the internet now.

People recognize you from that video. The band invites you backstage at their next show. Meet and greet. Photo op with the whole band. Signed merch with a personal message thanking you for being so into the music that night. All because you put your phone down and actually experienced the moment instead of filming an inferior version of what was already being captured.

You're trying to preserve the memory by filming it. But you're preventing the memory from forming.

That's a paradox. The act of documentation interferes with the experience you're trying to document.

You film the concert to remember being there. But you don't actually remember being there—you remember filming it.

Your Brain Needs You Present

Think about the last time someone told you a story while you were scrolling through social media.

Can you remember what they said? Probably not.

But you might remember the post you were reading.

That's not because you're a terrible listener or a terrible friend. Your brain can pay full attention to only one thing at a time.

There are several hypotheses that suggest the human brain cannot truly multitask when it comes to tasks that require conscious attention and focus. Instead, what we perceive as multitasking is actually task switching—where the brain rapidly shifts its attention back and forth between different activities. When you're scrolling, that's what your brain is encoding. That's what's getting saved as the memory.

When you're filming a concert on your phone, your brain is encoding the act of filming—the framing, the screen, whether you're getting the shot, keeping your hand steady. Not the actual music. Not the energy in the room. Not the experience of being there.

The moments you're absent for don't come back. You can't re-experience your kid's graduation. You can't re-attend that concert. You can't get another hour in the NICU.

Once they're gone, they're gone.

So when you divide your attention between your daughter's recital and your work email, you're not getting 50% of each experience. You're getting a degraded version of both. You're not present at either.

"But it's important!"

Who is? Your work or your daughter?

Your Distraction Affects Your Surroundings

Not only are you filming or distracting yourself from the present event, but you're also distracting others.

Walk into a movie theater after the lights go down.

Count the phone screens glowing in the dark. People checking messages. Scrolling through feeds. Responding to texts. Not watching the movie they paid to see.

But it's not just their experience they're ruining.

That phone screen is a flashlight in a dark room. It pulls everyone's eyes away from the screen. Breaks the immersion. Ruins the moment for the person next to them, behind them, in front of them.

Their distraction isn't their problem. It's everyone's problem.

The person beside them in the theater didn't pay to watch them scroll through Instagram. They paid to lose themselves in a story. And its phone glow yanks them out of it.

Same thing in real life. When you're scrolling during a conversation, the other person knows. They can feel it. They're trying to tell you something that matters to them, and you're signaling—without saying it—that whatever's on your screen matters more.

Your absence doesn't just affect you. It affects everyone trying to be present with you.

Your Kid Is Looking for You

You're going to your kid's school recital. It's graduation day, and they've prepared an event for the parents. The auditorium fills up. Kids file onto the stage in their caps and gowns, or their recital outfits, whatever the event calls for.

You find a seat. Pull out your phone to check one last work email before it starts. Then the ceremony begins, and you keep your phone in your lap. Just in case something urgent comes through. Or maybe you're scrolling. Or maybe you have your AirPods in, taking a work call you couldn't reschedule.

The kid is on stage. Scanning the crowd. Looking for their parents' eyes.

I know this because I've seen my kid's face when he finds us in the crowd. His expression changes. He's looking for that connection. That acknowledgment that we're watching, that we see him, that this moment matters to us too.

The kid doesn't know you're on an "important work call." They don't understand that your boss needed an answer right away, or that you're checking something urgent.

They just know you're not watching them.

They'll remember that you were there—technically. Physically present. In the room.

But they'll also remember that you weren't really there. That when they looked for you, when they wanted to see if you saw them, your attention was somewhere else.

That's the memory they're creating. Not because you're a terrible parent. Because you're human, and distraction is everywhere, and we've normalized being absent while present.

You're in the driver's seat of this relationship. Your kid is watching how you drive it.

The Content Already Exists

There's no exam on how much content you generate.

Nobody's grading you on your concert footage quality. Nobody's evaluating your vacation photos. Nobody's keeping score of how many moments you captured.

The content you're desperately trying to create? It already exists. Professional versions of it. Better versions than you could make with your phone.

What doesn't exist—what can't be replicated by anyone else—is your experience of being there.

Your perspective. Your presence. Your actual attention on what's happening in front of you.

That's what's unique. That's what's irreplaceable.

Not the footage. The experience itself.

And every moment you spend creating content about your life is a moment you're not actually living your life.

You're in the driver's seat. But instead of watching the road, you're filming it.

What You're Trading

I'm not saying you can never take a photo. Never record anything. Never share moments with people you care about.

But understand the trade you're making.

Every time you pull out your phone to capture something, you're trading presence for documentation. Experience for content. Being there for proving you were there.

Sometimes that trade makes sense. Sometimes you want the documentation more than you want the full experience in that moment.

But most of the time? We're not making a conscious choice. We're defaulting to documentation because everyone else is. Because we're afraid we'll forget. We think we need proof.

And we end up with thousands of photos we never look at and memories we never actually formed.

The phone in your lap during your kid's recital? That's not giving you anything. It's just taking you away from the moment.

The scrolling during your commute? You're watching other people's roads instead of driving your own.

The filming at the concert? You're preventing the very memory you're trying to preserve.

You're trading irreplaceable moments for... what, exactly? Content that already exists in a better form? Proof for people who weren't there and don't actually care that much?

Where Your Eyes Need to Be

The actual road you're driving. The actual moment you're in. The actual life you're living.

Not someone else's road. Not someone else's highlight reel. Not the professionally filmed version you're going to watch later instead of experiencing now.

Your road. Right now. This moment. Sometimes the scenic route IS the point.

Today isn't a countdown to better days. Today is your complete journey. Right now. This moment is part of your 100%.

And if you're not present for it—if your eyes are everywhere except the road you're actually driving—you're missing your own life.

Look around. Everything counts. Small gestures matter—including the barista who smiled at you this morning.

The guardrails help. The Waze horizontal. The phone in another room during dinner. The decision to just watch instead of film.

But it's a choice you make moment by moment.

Your kid is on stage looking for you. Are your eyes on them, or on your screen?

Your friend is telling you something important. Are you listening, or scrolling?

You're behind the wheel of your actual life. Are your eyes on your road, or someone else's?

There's no exam grading your presence. No scorecard tracking your attention. No final evaluation of whether you were really there for your own life.

But you'll know. In the quiet moments. In the memories you wish you had but don't. In the moments you were physically present for but completely missed.

You're driving this route. Nobody else can do it for you. Nobody else can be present for your moments. Nobody else can keep your eyes on your road.

That's your job.

Not because someone's watching. Because it's your road. Your life. Your one chance to actually be here for it.

Chapter 18

YOUR UNIQUE COMMUTE

Nobody in the history of the highway has driven or will ever drive your exact route.

This isn't fortune cookie wisdom. It's mathematical reality. The specific combination of where you started, which turns you made, what passengers you've carried, which rest stops you needed, which detours you took—that's unrepeatable.

Even if someone tried to replicate your journey step by step, they couldn't. Too many variables. Different timing. Different weather. Different version of themselves making the choices.

Your route is mathematically completely yours.

The Car Dealership Five Years Later

Picture a car dealership. Rows of identical vehicles fresh off the assembly line. Same make, same model, same year. Some indistinguishable except for paint color.

Ten people buy the same car on the same day.

Come back five years later. Line up those ten cars in the parking lot.

They don't look the same anymore.

One has 80,000 highway miles, smooth wear, minimal tear, consistent maintenance. One has 40,000 city miles, stop-and-go traffic damage, worn brakes, and stress from constant acceleration and deceleration. One has 100,000 miles of gravel roads and mountain passes, undercarriage rust, suspension work, character marks from terrain.

Same car. Completely different journeys. And each journey left its mark.

You can see which one belonged to the parent shuttling kids to school every morning. Which one belonged to the sales rep driving interstates. Which one belonged to the weekend adventurer taking back roads through national parks.

The cars started identical. The routes made them different.

You might have started from a similar place as someone else—same hometown, same school, same opportunities. But the specific route you drove, the specific choices you made at each intersection, the specific passengers you carried, the specific terrain you navigated—all of that created the unrepeatable version of you that exists right now.

Even Twins Diverge

Let's take again the identical twins example. Genetically the same. Raised in the same house, by the same parents, in the same culture, eating the same food, attending the same schools.

As similar as two human starting points can possibly be.

And they still end up different people.

One becomes an artist. One becomes an engineer. One moves across the country. One stays in their hometown. One marries early. One stays single. One has kids. One doesn't.

Not just distinct personalities—that's expected. Even if we lived in a world where only looks mattered for opportunities, where attractive people got all the job offers and interviews, identical twins still wouldn't receive the same opportunities. Same face, but one walks into the office on the day they're hiring. The other walks in a week later when the position's filled. Or one gets noticed by a recruiter at a coffee shop. The other was at home that day. Same appearance, different timing, completely different outcomes.

Why? Because even though they started from the same place, they didn't drive the same route.

Maybe one got sick as a kid and spent months in the hospital—that changed everything about how they see health, risk, mortality. Maybe one had a teacher who sparked something. Maybe one made a friend who pulled them in a different direction. Maybe one chose left at an intersection where the other chose right, and that single turn cascaded into completely different decades.

If identical twins can't replicate each other's routes, what chance does anyone else have of replicating yours?

Your Background Is Unrepeatable

You didn't just start from a place. You started from a specific moment in time, with specific circumstances, with specific people around you, with a specific version of the world that doesn't exist anymore.

The economic reality you entered. The technology available. The cultural values your generation absorbed. The opportunities that existed or didn't exist. The specific family dynamics you navigated. The exact sequence of experiences that shaped how you process everything else.

Someone born ten years before you? Different world. Different rules. Different baseline assumptions about what's possible.

Someone born ten years after you? Also different. Technologies you had to learn, they were born into. Your fear and struggles, some they don't even understand. Advantages they have, you never had access to.

Even someone born the same year as you, in the same city, from a similar background, still didn't have your parents. Your siblings. Your teachers. Your random encounters. Your specific sequence of failures and successes that taught you what you know now.

Your starting point was unique. Your route through the years has been unique. And the version of you that resulted from all of that? Also unique.

Not better. Not worse. Just unrepeatable.

Navigation Styles Are Part of It

And it's not just the external circumstances. It's how YOU navigate them.

Some people drive defensively, always anticipating problems, planning three moves ahead, protecting against worst-case scenarios. Some people drive intuitively, deciding in the moment, trusting their instincts, adapting as they go. Some drive ruthlessly, trying to own the road, even doing it with anger. Some people drive analytically, researching every route, optimizing for efficiency, calculating trade-offs.

None of those styles are wrong. They're just different ways of moving through life. And your style is part of what makes your route unrepeatable.

Even if someone else faced the exact same intersection you faced, they wouldn't navigate it the way you did. Because they're not you. They don't have your specific combination of caution and courage, logic and emotion, planning and spontaneity.

Your route isn't just WHERE you've driven. It's HOW you've driven it.

Look at those ten cars from the dealership. Each one needed a different maintenance schedule. Different driving styles. Different routes that matched their usage. What worked for the highway car would destroy the mountain pass car. What worked for the city car wouldn't serve the cross-country car.

Your route is specific. Your circumstances are specific. Your navigation style is specific.

What worked for someone else might completely fail on yours.

That doesn't mean you did something wrong. It means their route wasn't yours.

You Are the Standard for Your Journey

And because your route is unique, YOU are the only valid standard for YOUR journey.

Not because your way is better than everyone else's. But because no one else had your exact set of choices. They didn't face your specific terrain. They didn't navigate your specific weather. They didn't start from your specific location or carry your specific passengers.

When you compare your progress to someone else's, you're comparing incompatible measurements. They're measuring miles driven on completely different terrain. Their odometer reading has nothing to do with yours. It's like comparing your desert route to their coastal highway—same distance traveled, completely unique experiences, completely unique challenges.

You can learn from them. You can be inspired by them. You may adapt principles from their navigation style.

But you can't use their route as proof that yours is wrong.

They weren't driving YOUR car, on YOUR roads, with YOUR passengers, facing YOUR weather, making YOUR decisions.

You are the only person who had your route. Which means you are the only valid measure of whether you're navigating it well.

Can't Live Fully While Driving Someone Else's Route

When you try to follow someone else's route instead of your own, when you measure your journey against theirs, or force your route to theirs, here's how that plays out:

You stress about not being where they were at your age. I know—it's hard to stop comparing. You feel behind. You feel you're failing because your odometer doesn't match theirs. But you're not behind. You're on a different route entirely, measuring your progress against someone who started from a different place, faced different terrain, and was heading somewhere else. Their timeline has nothing to do with yours.

You try to force your circumstances to match theirs. You make choices that don't fit your actual situation because "that's what they did, and it worked for them." You take a job you hate because it's the "right" career path. You buy things you can't afford because that's what success is supposed to look like. You push yourself into situations that feel wrong because their route says this is where you should be by now.

But forcing their map onto your terrain doesn't work. You just end up stressed, exhausted, suffering, and still not where you thought you'd be.

You ignore what actually matters to YOU because you're too busy trying to achieve what mattered to THEM. You spend years climbing a ladder that's leaning against the wrong building. You optimize for outcomes that look impressive on someone else's route map but feel completely empty on yours. And you end up living a life that photographs well but doesn't feel like it belongs to you.

You can't live fully while trying to drive someone else's route. Their route wasn't designed for your vehicle, your terrain, your destination, your style. It was designed for theirs. And no amount of effort will make their route fit your journey.

Drive YOUR route. Period. This is the way—YOUR way. With all its unique turns and specific circumstances and unrepeatable combinations.

That's not settling. That's not giving up.

Your route is yours. And trying to navigate someone else's won't get you anywhere meaningful.

The Wholeness Matters

Your perspective is unique. Your memories are yours alone. Your context shapes everything you experience.

But the reason your route is unique goes beyond any single element.

It's the WHOLENESS of your journey. The way everything compounds together.

Not just one element. The entire combination. The way everything interacts with everything else to create the specific version of life you're living right now.

Your background shaped your perspective. Your perspective influenced your choices. Your choices created your circumstances. Your circumstances shaped your next set of choices. All of it compounding, layering, creating something that could only have happened exactly this way.

That's why trying to replicate someone else's journey doesn't work.

You're not clones. You can't copy someone's route and expect the same results. You can copy individual choices, but you can't copy the entire web of factors that made those choices make sense for them. Their background, their perspective, their circumstances, their timing, all interact in ways that don't transfer to your situation.

You Are Ready

You've been on the road for seventeen stretches now. You have learned things. You have unlearned things. You've seen how the highway works, how other drivers navigate their routes, how the rules keep us from crashing into each other.

You've looked in the rearview mirror at where you came from. You've recognized the programming you inherited. You've understood that comparison is pointless and competition doesn't work for you.

You've seen that other people aren't NPCs. That today is 100% of your life, not a countdown to something better. That your eyes need to be on YOUR road, not everyone else's.

And now you understand why all of that matters: because your route is mathematically, completely yours.

No one else can drive it for you. No one else can tell you whether you're doing it right or wrong. No one else had your exact starting point, your exact circumstances, your exact sequence of decisions.

Which means no one else gets to grade your journey. And more importantly, you can stop looking for that grade. Stop wondering whether you're measuring up. Stop seeking validation that you're doing it "correctly." There's no external scorecard. There's no judge reviewing your route and deciding if it's good enough. No one else's route proves yours is insufficient. No one else's odometer reading makes yours less valid.

Your route is yours.

Learning from the terrain. Understanding which passengers to carry. Recognizing when your pace needs to shift.

Not because someone taught you the "right" way to do those things. Because you learned by doing them.

You're not waiting for someone else to allow you to drive your life. Do it.

You're already driving it. The pull to be present is strong. Give in to it. Let it be with you.

And now you understand why your specific route, with all its unique turns and unrepeatable combinations, is the only route that could have brought you here.

There is no exam grading whether you chose the "correct" route compared to everyone else's.

There's just your route. Your journey can't be measured against anyone else's because the circumstances are incomparable.

And you're ready to keep driving it.

THIRD PIT STOP

You just drove through the best stretch of highway yet.

Part Six wasn't about unlearning or examining or understanding anymore. This part was about actually living.

Today isn't a countdown—it's 100% of your life. Your eyes need to be on your own road, not everyone else's. And your route is uniquely yours. Not as inspiration. Fact.

So pull over one more time. Last pit stop before the last stretch.

Look how differently you're driving compared to when you left your neighborhood. You're not racing anyone. You're not comparing your odometer to everyone else's. You're not trying to win a competition that never existed.

You've unlearned the programming from your hometown. You've recognized that other people aren't obstacles or NPCs—they're travelers on their own routes. You've understood that the journey itself IS the life you're living, not preparation for something else.

And now you're ready for something you might not have expected when we started this drive.

Part Seven differs from everything before it. The previous parts were about seeing clearly—understanding how things actually work, recognizing what you've been carrying, validating why your route is yours.

This last part? It's about what you do with this clarity.

No instructions. Not a checklist. Not BS like: "here's the 5 steps to living without an exam."

Just some observations about what driving your own route actually looks like when you stop waiting for permission. When you stop measuring against everyone else. When you take full ownership of the wheel you've been holding this entire time.

You've been driving for eighteen chapters. You know how this works now.

These last few chapters are about driving with intention. With ownership. Understanding that this commute—this route, this journey, this life—is completely, entirely, yours to navigate.

Ready for the last stretch? I am.

Let's finish this drive.

Part Seven

TAKING THE WHEEL

Gradually taking more control.

Chapter 19

RACING YOUR OWN ODOMETER

On this open stretch of highway, something shifts. You're not checking your rearview mirror to see who's behind you. You're not watching the cars ahead trying to catch up. You're looking at your own dashboard. Your own odometer. Your own gauge showing how far you've come.

Same highway. Different question. No more "Are we there yet?" Not "Am I ahead of them?" but "How far can I push this?"

Part Seven starts here. Everything before this was about seeing clearly—understanding the highway, recognizing what you've been carrying, watching how other drivers navigate their own routes. You've done that work. You've pulled over at rest stops, examined your trunk, left some things behind.

Now comes the part where you actually drive your way.

Not because someone's grading your performance. Not because you need to prove you're better than the car next to you. But because you want to see what your car can do. How far you can push yourself. What you're actually capable of when you stop measuring against everyone else and start measuring against your own baseline.

This isn't about racing. This is about reaching.

The Mountain You Climb

People say, "I conquered the mountain."

No, you didn't. The mountain's still there. It didn't surrender. It didn't lose. It'll be there long after you're gone, exactly the same height, completely indifferent to whether you reached the top.

What you conquered was yourself. Your doubt. Your fear. Your body's signals telling you to stop. The voice in your head saying, "This is good enough, can we turn back now?"

The mountain was just the terrain. You were the opponent.

Same thing with your route. You're not trying to beat the other drivers. You're trying to beat yesterday's version of yourself. The only competition is with yesterday's you. The one who drove 1,000 miles in total. Today you're at 1,050. Fifty miles further than you've ever been. That's the competition that actually matters.

Every time you push past where you were yesterday, you're competing against your own previous standard. Not anyone else's. Yours. Yesterday was good. Today can be even better.

And this differs from the competition you unlearned back at the rest area: this competition makes you better instead of making you bitter.

How Far Can You Go

The question isn't "How long will this take?" The question is, "How far can I actually go?"

John C. Maxwell explains this amazingly in his book *Leadershift*, when he's talking about shifting from goals to growth:

> As I made this shift, instead of worrying about how long something might take, I started asking, How far can I go? Instead of thinking about what I was getting and how much I had to pay to get it, I started to think about who I was becoming and the impact I could make because of it. I recognized I was on a growth journey.[1]

Not racing the clock. Not racing other drivers. Just seeing what your car is capable of. What you're capable of. What happens when you stop comparing your route to everyone else's and start asking yourself: "What can I do better than I did yesterday?"

Maybe yesterday you drove patiently. Today you drove with patience AND you let three cars merge without getting frustrated. Progress.

Maybe yesterday you stayed present during dinner with your family. Today you stayed present AND you put your phone in another room. Progress.

Maybe yesterday you worked on your project for an hour. Today you worked for an hour AND you pushed past the part where you usually give up. Progress.

None of that required beating anyone else. None of that required being ranked. None of that needed external validation. You don't have to aim "to the moon" to make progress.

You just needed to know: how can I go further than I went yesterday?

That's competing against yourself. Your past self is challenging you: "Catch me if you can."

Championships Aren't Goals

Imagine you've been playing tennis since you were young. Recreational, not professional, but you enjoy it. You're good at it. But now you want to take it to the next level. You've entered a semi-pro tournament—something you've always wanted to try.

So you train. Every day after work, you're on the court. Some days you stay late to practice your volley. Some days you work on your serve until your shoulder aches. You're doing everything you can because you want to win that trophy.

Except the championship doesn't depend entirely on you.

A bad call from the chair umpire can ruin your match. Your opponent might just outperform you—they're not an NPC in your story: they trained just as hard as you did, worked just as long, same as you. Or the opposite, maybe you win because your opponent made two big, inconceivable errors. Not because you played better than them, but because your win is relative to their performance on that specific day.

You can control your training. You can control your effort. You can control whether you show up and give everything you have.

You cannot control the outcome.

The championship is not the objective. It's a consequence.

Even professional sports teams understand this. But fans demand trophies. They want guarantees. Coaches know they can't promise that —they know too many variables are out of their control—but even knowing that, they have to stand in front of cameras and declare that their only objective is clearly the trophy. That's what sells tickets. That's what keeps fans invested. That's what gives them hope.

But behind closed doors? The focus is different. They can control only what they can control. If everyone on the team does what they're supposed to do, if they execute the fundamentals, if they play well enough—the wins will start showing up. Not as something they forced into existence. As something that happened because they did their part well.

Your "championships" might happen because of the work. Or they might not, because a hundred variables outside your control are also in play.

But either way, you became someone stronger, more capable, wise, more experienced than you were when you started. The external reward is a consequence. The internal growth gets logged on your odometer.

The Greatest in the World

Let's say you've found your thing. Maybe it's woodworking. Maybe it's coding. Maybe it's photography. You love it, you're good at it, and you want to keep getting better.

So naturally, you think: I'm gonna be the best at this. The greatest in the world.

But remember back in Chapter 6, when we talked about what would happen if everyone disappeared? If everyone better than you was suddenly gone, you'd be "the greatest"... and it would mean nothing. The title would be hollow.

Because "the best in the world" is a moving target you can't control. It depends on who shows up, what they bring, and what advantages they have that you don't. You're measuring yourself against people whose circumstances, resources, and starting points differ completely from yours.

But yesterday's you? That's a fixed point. You know exactly where you were. You know exactly what you were capable of. You have complete data about your previous performance.

Your goal should be to be greater than your version from the day before. That's it.

The Age Label You Don't Need

Let's say you hit 40 years old. Welcome to the fourth floor. Now you're "Halfway through your life," "Middle age," "Over the hill," "Not young anymore."

But now you know you're at your 100%. You know that the "old" tag is relative. Put yourself in Okinawa, Japan, surrounded by people in their 90s. Do you feel old at 40? Of course not. You will feel young around them.

So if the feeling is relative—if it changes depending on who's around you—why are you labeling yourself as if it's absolute?

The programming to feel old at certain ages is just that: programming. Something you learned. Something your culture taught you. Not reality.

You're not old. You're not young. You're just at the mileage you're at. And tomorrow you'll have more miles. And the day after that, more still.

And if you need a label, here it is: you're young.

There's always an older group than you on the planet. You're just in the wrong spot for the comparison.

Life Is Like a Song

Our goal should be to enjoy life while it's being played, not to reach the end.

Think about listening to a song you love. You don't sit there thinking, "I can't wait to hear the final chord of this song." You don't measure its value by whether it reaches the ending. You experience it. You let it unfold. You appreciate each measure as it comes.

The point of the song isn't the last note. The point is the melody, the rhythm, the way it makes you feel while it's playing.

Same with your route. The point isn't to accumulate as many accomplishments as possible before you reach the end. The point isn't to rush through your life checking boxes—"whatever it takes" to say you did everything before the song stops.

The point is to drive in a way that makes the journey worth taking.

Competing against yourself means making each stretch of highway better than the last one. More intentional. More present. More aligned with who you actually want to be behind that wheel.

Not racing to the end. Just driving better than you drove yesterday, and making stops when you want, even if others didn't stop.

Do You Need or Do You Want the Expensive Car?

We notice people buying expensive products all the time. Sometimes to buy status, to get validation. But sometimes that's not the reason at all—and you know what? That's perfectly valid!

You're driving down this highway right now. You look at your dashboard, at your steering wheel, and you remember your childhood dream about someday driving the special car you wanted as a kid. It's expensive.

But hey, now you CAN afford it. It makes sense in your life. The purchase won't put you in financial trouble. Your family supports it—do it.

Go ahead. Spoil yourself.

This is your life.

Not to show off. Not to gain admiration. Not to prove anything to anyone else. Get it because you want it. Because it makes you happy. Because it's part of your route.

The car won't define you. You've already defined yourself in your current branch of the tree. You don't need a car to make you valuable or important or successful. Those things are already true about you, or they're not, regardless of what you drive.

But if that car brings you joy? If driving it makes your commute better? If you worked hard, and this is something you've wanted for yourself? That's reason enough.

This is competing against yourself too. Not the version of you who bought things for other people's approval. The version of you who knows what you actually want and goes after it.

Your destinations are yours. Your goals are yours. Your definition of "better" is yours.

The car is just an example. This applies to everything you've always wanted to do with your life. But also what you don't want.

REMOVING WHAT YOU DON'T ACTUALLY WANT

Mo Gawdat, in his book *Solve For Happy*, puts it clearly:

> Happiness is the absence of unhappiness. It's our resting state when nothing clouds the picture or causes interference. Happiness is *your* default state.[2]

You're not trying to add things to become happy. You're already happy. That's your default. You don't need to achieve things to be happy. You don't need to add milestones, accomplishments, or validations. You need to remove the things that are making you unhappy right now so you can return to your default state.

I told you about the Air Jordan collecting—the 4am bidding, the 34 pairs, the imaginary deadline. But I didn't tell you why I was doing it. I wasn't collecting because I loved every pair. I was collecting to show everybody. To prove something.

I thought being first in line buying the next one out would make me happy. The best collector.

I wasn't collecting—I was pulling a heist on my own happiness.

Same thing with Star Wars collectibles. Lightsabers, helmets, tons of them. Not because I loved each one, but because I had this urge to have them all.

Now? I've sold most of them. I still keep the ones I love—not the ones everyone loves and because of THAT I got them in the first place. The ones I actually love.

I added nothing to become happy. I removed the compulsion to acquire them, the need to have "more," the pressure to keep up with what everyone else was collecting.

The bigger thought I removed? That I was thinking there was an exam. That I wanted to show everybody and please everyone always. That made me stressed and unhappy. I was in constant validation mode. Now, I'm trying my best not to be afraid anymore.

I learned to say no. I learned that what I achieve is for me, not for others to compare or validate me.

That's what competing against yourself actually means. Not "how much can I accumulate to impress others?" but "what do I actually want for me?"

Your achievements don't need external validation. Your progress doesn't need other people's approval. You have nothing to fear. You're not racing to prove anything to anyone watching.

You're racing your own odometer. And sometimes that means removing things, not adding them. Sometimes getting better than yesterday's you means letting go of what yesterday's you thought mattered.

The expensive car? Get it if YOU want it. The collection? Keep what YOU love. The goal? Chase it because YOU chose it.

Not because there's a leaderboard tracking your performance. Not because someone's grading your choices. Not because you need to prove you're better than the version of you other people expected.

Just because you decided this is what matters on your route.

Not racing anyone. Not proving anything. Just seeing how far you can actually go when you stop comparing and start competing with the only person whose performance you can actually measure: yesterday's you.

There is no exam grading whether you beat everyone else.

There's just your odometer, yesterday's number, and today's question: how far can I go?

Chapter 20

YOUR HANDS ON YOUR WHEEL

M aybe you've noticed something by now: the highway has a lot of things you can't do anything about.

You can't control the weather. You can't control construction zones. You can't control whether the driver ahead of you suddenly brakes for no reason. You can't control traffic, accidents, road closures, or the fact that everyone merged onto the highway at exactly the same time you did.

But you can control your steering wheel.

That's not a small thing. That's everything.

The Steering Wheel Reality

You control where you point your car. How you react when someone cuts you off. Whether you speed up, slow down, or change lanes. Your hands, your feet, your attention, your decisions.

The highway doesn't care what you want. The other drivers aren't coordinating with you. The conditions aren't waiting for your approval.

But your steering wheel? That's yours.

And that's where your energy belongs—on what you can actually influence, not on what you wish you could control but never will.

Imagine you're driving through a construction zone. Two lanes merge into one. Traffic slows to a crawl. You're going to be late.

What can you control?

You can't control that the construction exists. You can't control that everyone else is also stuck in this merge. You can't control how fast the car ahead of you is moving.

But you can control whether you get frustrated or accept it. Whether you honk aggressively or let someone merge in front of you. Whether you make the situation worse by tailgating and stress-driving, or whether you just drive through it.

Same construction zone. Same traffic. Completely different experiences based on what you chose to control.

Allowing Change, Not Forcing It

Change happens whether or not you're ready.

Your body ages. Your industry evolves. Your city changes. Your relationships shift. Technology advances. Your priorities realign.

You can't stop any of that. You can't freeze time at a point when everything felt perfect. You can't force things to stay the way they were just because you liked them that way.

Change doesn't ask for your permission. It doesn't wait for you to approve. It just happens.

That's maturity. Recognizing that you don't control whether change happens. You only control whether you allow it or resist it.

Resisting change doesn't stop it. It just makes you miserable while it happens, anyway. You spend your energy fighting against something inevitable, trying to hold on to a version of reality that's already gone.

Allowing change doesn't mean you're giving up. It means you're recognizing what's actually in your control.

If you have kids, you can't control that they're going to become teenagers with their own opinions and priorities. But you can control whether you fight against who they're becoming or make space for them to grow.

You can't control that your company is restructuring. But you can control whether you spend your energy resisting it or adapting to the new reality.

You can't control that your neighborhood is now different from how it was ten years ago. But you can control whether you stay bitter about what's gone or find what's valuable in what's here now.

You don't create change. You don't force it. You allow it.

That's your steering wheel with change. You control your response, your adaptation, whether you accept what's inevitable or waste your energy trying to prevent it.

Change is going to happen. The highway is going to have construction zones, detours, new routes. You don't control that.

But you control how you navigate it.

The Hospital Log

One time, my wife was hospitalized in a very delicate state.

It's hard to watch the love of your life hooked to a bed, feeling pain you can't take away. Everything in you wants to do something. Fix it. Make it stop.

I could have lost it. Easily. Sat in that chair spiraling into worst-case scenarios. Started crying on the inside, thinking about what might happen.

But I didn't. Because none of that would help her.

I'm not a doctor. I can't diagnose. I can't prescribe. I can't control whether the right specialist is on duty, whether the nurses catch every signal, whether the doctor stuck in traffic arrives in time.

But I can log.

I started documenting. Every blood pressure reading. Every time a monitor beeped. Every signal, every number, timestamped on my phone. Not because I knew what any of it meant—but because when the doctor arrived, I could hand them a complete picture. "Here's everything that happened in the last four hours."

I couldn't control her health. I couldn't control the hospital. But I could be complementary to the people who could.

That's the shift. You stop trying to control things outside your scope and start asking: what am I actually capable of doing right now? What's the steering wheel I can hold?

My wife needed me present, not panicking. The doctors needed data, not interference. And I needed something to do with all that fear besides let it consume me.

So I logged. Timestamp by timestamp. That was my steering wheel. And that helped the doctors.

So let's look at how this plays out in your actual life. Where the steering wheel is actually in your hands. Where you get to decide what you focus your energy on.

At Work

Many people work in fear.

Fear of getting fired. Fear of not being good enough. Fear of losing their jobs if they make a mistake or don't perform perfectly.

But here's how I see it: the company is investing in me.

They're giving me a job, a salary, an opportunity to grow and be part of something bigger. And I'm going to take advantage of that investment. Not selfishly—in a smart way. I'm going to learn. I'm going to grow professionally at a pace I could never achieve alone, without a company supporting me.

If tomorrow were my last day, I want to make the most of today. I want to inspire my colleagues. I want to push creative boundaries. I want to focus on my growth, which consequently benefits the company.

That order has a reason. I'm not focusing on the company's growth (that's relative). I'm focusing on my growth (my objective), which helps the company (as a consequence). Those parentheses sound familiar?

That's what I can control. My effort. My learning. My contribution. My attitude. I'm a man of my word—and my word is to focus on what I can control.

I can't control whether the company decides to let me go or not. I can't control market conditions, layoffs, restructures, or budget cuts. I can't control whether my manager likes me or whether my project gets funding.

But I can control whether I show up and do work I'm proud of. Whether I take advantage of the resources they're giving me. Whether I grow into someone more capable than I was yesterday. Today I am at the 100% of my tenure.

That's my steering wheel at work. Everything else is traffic conditions.

The People You Choose

You can't control how your friends react to you.

Whether they like you. Whether they'll be there when you need them. But you can control with whom you share things.

Who you tell your secrets to. Who you ask for advice. Who you invite into your experiences. Who you trust with the parts of yourself that matter.

You're choosing your passengers. And that's huge.

Why? Because maybe you have a friend who's great for laughing with, but so terrible with serious conversations. You can't control their behaviour—that's just who they are (and they aren't NPCs). But you can control whether you try to have deep, vulnerable conversations with them and then feel hurt when they don't show up the way you need.

Maybe you've got a friend who's amazing at giving practical advice but awful at emotional support. You can't change that. But you can control whether you go to them when you need a hug or when you need help problem-solving.

You're not controlling their reactions. You're controlling who gets access to what parts of your journey. You decide who rides shotgun and who gets invited along on specific trips.

Same applies to romantic relationships.

You can't make someone fall in love with you. You can't force your crush to like you back. You can't manipulate someone into wanting to be with you. You can't force that kind of connection. You can't pressure someone into a relationship just because you set up some big public proposal that puts them on the spot in front of a crowd, making them feel like they have to say yes because everyone's watching.

That's not love. You're not even thinking about their feelings.

And you can't drive or control their feelings. You never will.

But you can control how you show up. Whether you're transparent. Whether you communicate honestly. Whether you show the best parts of yourself—not a fake version, not a performance, just the genuine you without pretending to be someone you're not.

If you're in a relationship, you can control how you take care of your partner. How you make them feel seen, heard, understood. How you encourage them. How you support them.

You can't control how they react. Whether they reciprocate. Whether they stay or leave.

But you can control the type of partner you are. The type of energy you bring. The type of attention you give.

That's your steering wheel with the people you choose. Drive it well, but don't grab theirs.

Family

Your parents—the people who raised you—they're getting older. You can't control their health, their time, or the fact that they're going to need more help, more care, more support as they age.

But you can control being there when they do. You can control ensuring they're not helpless and alone. You can control giving them dignity and care when they need it most.

If you share your life with your partner, their family becomes part of your world. Their parents, siblings, extended network—they're all connected to you now through the person you care about.

You can't control whether they like you or not. Whether they accept you immediately or take years to warm up to you. Their opinions, their judgments, their comments at family gatherings.

But you can control how you treat them. You can make them feel like family. You can honor the trust they showed when they welcomed you into their lives—they're sharing someone they love with you.

You can't make them see you in a certain way. But you can be someone worth seeing.

If you have kids, you can control how good of a parent you are: being a role model, being present, patient, intentional.

You can't control how they turn out, the choices they make as they grow up, or whether they remember you the way you hope they will.

But you can control showing up. Being there. Driving in a way that gives them something worth remembering.

That's your steering wheel with family. You don't control their reactions or their outcomes. You control your actions and your presence.

In Daily Life

You can't control traffic. But you can let the three cars merge in front of you without getting frustrated, making their commute a little less stressful.

You can't make people like you. But you can say good morning to three different people and brighten their day expecting nothing back.

You can't control the person behind you. But you can hold the door for them, a tiny gesture that costs you nothing and makes the world slightly better.

You can't control whether people respect you. But you can be respectful, even when it's not returned.

You can't control whether your day goes well. But you can make someone else's day go better.

You can't control how long your pets are going to live. But you can control how to give them a pet-worthy life.

None of this is about being a saint. None of this is about performing kindness for credit. This is just about recognizing the steering wheel is in your hands. You get to decide how you drive.

Every interaction is a choice. Every reaction is a decision. Every moment where you could make things worse or make things better—that's your steering wheel. Put a smile on your face.

You control that.

Your steering wheel. Your lane. Your actions.

That's where the competition with yesterday's you actually happens. Not by controlling the highway. By controlling how you drive on it.

Chapter 21

HOW YOU DROVE MATTERS

After all these miles, what you've been building without realizing it is not a trophy. Not a monument. Not a collection of achievements to point at when someone asks what you've accomplished.

What you've been building is influence.

Not the kind that shows up in your will. Not the kind that gets divided among heirs. Not the kind that wears out or depreciates or gets sold at an estate sale.

The kind that stays with people long after you've stopped driving.

Taking the wheel means taking charge of your legacy—what you're leaving in people right now, not what you'll leave for them later.

The Car or the Driving

You could leave your kid your car. Title transferred, keys handed over, vehicle in their name. That's inheritance. That's something FOR them.

Or you could teach them how you drove it. How you handled tough roads. How you stayed patient in traffic. How you navigated when you didn't know the route. How you made decisions when the weather turned bad. Pass it down.

That's legacy. That's something IN them.

Anyone can buy a car. Not everyone gets to learn from the driver who taught them how to handle one.

The car will eventually break down. It'll need repairs, then more repairs, then one day it won't be worth fixing anymore. That's just how cars work.

But the way you taught them to drive? That stays. That becomes part of how they navigate their own route. That influences how they'll drive for the rest of their lives.

That's not something you can leave in a will. That's something they carry because they rode with you.

What Actually Transfers

Money transfers. Property transfers. Possessions transfer.

But those things can't show your someone how to stay calm when everything feels chaotic. They can't teach your friend how to think through a problem from a different angle. They can't give your partner the feeling of being truly seen and understood.

Those things? Those only transfer through presence. Through the time you spent riding together. Through the moments when they watched how you handled something and thought, "That's how I want to handle it too."

Your parents probably left you things. Maybe a house, maybe some savings, maybe family heirlooms. And those things might have been helpful, might have been meaningful.

But what do you actually carry from them?

You carry the way your mom stayed calm during emergencies. You carry the way your dad approached problems methodically. You carry the values they lived, not the ones they talked about. You carry the lessons they showed you through how they drove, not the lectures they gave you about how you should drive.

The physical things? Those are nice. But they're not the legacy.

Their legacy is IN you. In how you think. In how you react. In how you navigate your own route.

The Inheritance Everyone Can Buy

Possessions wear out. Money runs out. Things break, depreciate, get lost, get stolen, become obsolete.

That inheritance you got? It served a purpose. It helped. But if it was just money or property, someone else could have given you the same thing.

What someone else couldn't give you? The specific way your parents thought. The particular approach they had to life. The unique perspective they brought to problems. The way they made you feel capable even when you doubted yourself.

That's irreplaceable. That's what actually matters.

The material inheritance? it equalizes. Give ten people each $100,000 and they all have the same amount of money. The transaction is identical.

But influence? Influence is unique. The way you affected someone's thinking, the way you changed how they see themselves, the way you influenced their route—that's something only you could give them. Nobody else has your exact combination of experiences, perspectives, and presence.

That's an inheritance that lasts.

What Would You Prefer?

If I could choose, I'd rather my parents sell that luxury car now—grab whatever they've been saving—and use that money for themselves. It's their money. They earned it. They deserve to enjoy it.

Maybe that means traveling. Maybe it means finally doing that thing they always talked about. Maybe it means a road trip they've been postponing for decades. We're welcome to join if they want us there—but it's their run. Their route. Their miles to drive however they want.

Whatever brings them joy while they're still here to experience it.

When they're gone, I'm not going to treasure "the luxury car." I will not drive it thinking, "I'm so glad they saved this for me." I'm going to be selling it and trying to figure out what to do with all the stuff they left behind.

But watching them actually live? Seeing them enjoy what they built instead of just preserving it for us? That stays with me.

Watching my kid see their grandparents not as people who saved everything for later, but as people who knew how to live while they still could.

That's the inheritance I cherish.

Not the house with stuff I'll end up throwing away. Not the luxury car I'll sell because it doesn't fit my life. But the memory of seeing them happy. The proof that they didn't just work their whole lives to leave things behind—they actually enjoyed the ride.

That's what I'd choose for them. Every time.

Because possessions get divided, sold, lost, forgotten. But those experiences? Those become part of how I remember them. Those become part of what I carry. Those become part of what I tell my kid about who their grandparents were.

That's their legacy. Not what they left FOR me, but what they left IN me.

You're a Passenger in Their Journey

Here's another flip. You've been thinking about the passengers in your car. The people riding with you. The different versions of yourself they've experienced.

But you're also a passenger in someone else's car.

If you have kids, their journey isn't yours to drive. You're riding with them, but you're not driving. What matters is who's behind the wheel. And it's not you.

You're in the passenger seat, maybe offering directions, maybe pointing out things they haven't noticed, but ultimately they're the ones controlling where the car goes.

Same with your partner. Your friends. Your coworkers. Anyone in your life.

You don't drive their route. You ride along for part of it. Sometimes you're there for years. Sometimes just for a few miles. But you're never in their driver's seat—that's theirs alone.

What you can do is influence how they drive.

The confidence they feel navigating their route? You affected that.

The way they handle obstacles? You showed them approaches they might not have considered.

The patience they bring to tough stretches? They learned some of that from watching you.

You didn't drive for them. You drove WITH them. And that made their driving different from what it would have been without you.

That's YOUR legacy in their journey.

The Odometer That Stays

When someone's drive ends, their odometer doesn't disappear.

Think about that for a second. When someone you love stops driving—when they park for the last time—all those miles they traveled, all those routes they took, all that distance they covered... it doesn't just vanish.

It remains. In everyone who rode with them.

You're still carrying miles your loved ones drove. Routes they showed you. Turns they taught you to take. Ways of thinking they passed along during long drives together. Each generation better than the last.

They're not driving anymore. But their mileage is still accumulating —in you. In how you drive. In the choices you make. In the routes you take, because they showed you those roads existed.

Their odometer stayed. Their influence continues.

That's not metaphorical. That's not a comforting philosophy to make death feel less final. That's just what actually happens when you've truly influenced someone.

You become part of how they navigate the rest of their drive.

How You Made Them Feel

Your friend won't remember every conversation you had. Your kid won't remember every piece of advice you gave. Your partner won't remember every date you planned.

But they'll remember how you made them feel.

Did you make them feel capable? Did you make them feel seen? Did you make them feel like they could handle whatever road they were on?

Or did you make them feel inadequate? Constantly compared? Like they were always falling short?

That feeling—that's what sticks. That becomes part of how they see themselves. That's what influences their drive for years after you've stopped riding with them.

You might have given them a car. You might have paid for their education. You might have left them money.

But if you made them feel incompetent while doing it? If you made them feel like nothing they did was ever good enough? If you made them feel like they were constantly being measured and found wanting?

What you left behind isn't the car or the degree or the inheritance. Your legacy is that feeling.

And that's the one that lasts.

The Passengers You've Already Influenced

You've been driving for years. Decades, probably. And all that time, you've had passengers.

People have been in your car, watching how you handle stress. Watching how you react when things go wrong. Watching how you treat other drivers. Watching how you navigate when you're lost.

If you have kids, they watched you grip the steering wheel too tight when money was scarce. They absorbed that anxiety, whether or not you talked about it.

If you have a partner, they watched you handle conflict—whether you stayed calm or escalated, whether you listened or defended. That showed them something about how disagreements work in your shared life.

Your friends watched how you talked about people who weren't there. Whether you were kind or critical. Whether you could be trusted with sensitive information or whether everything became gossip.

You were teaching them the whole time. Not through lectures. Through presence. Through example. Through the version of yourself that showed up when you thought nobody paid that much attention.

They were paying attention.

And now they're driving with some of what you showed them.

That's already your legacy. It's already happening. You're already leaving something IN the people around you.

The only question is: what are you leaving?

You Can't Control Their Memory

Remember the earlier part of this drive where we talked about memories belonging to other people? How you can't control what they remember or how they remember it.

The same applies here.

You can't force people to remember you in a certain way. You can't write the script for how you'll live on in their minds. You can't control whether they focus on your best moments or your worst ones.

Their memory of you is theirs. Their experience of riding with you is theirs. The version of you they carry forward is their version, not your corrected one.

But what you can control: who you are while you're driving.

You can control your presence. You can control whether you're patient or reactive. You can control whether you make people feel capable or inadequate. You can control whether your passengers leave your car better for having ridden with you.

You can't control what they remember. But you can control what you give them to remember.

And that matters more than you think.

The Departed You Still Drive With

You're not alone in your car right now. You know that, right?

Everyone who influenced you—everyone who showed you how to handle certain roads, who taught you approaches you still use, who gave you perspectives you still carry—is still riding with you.

Your grandfather, who taught you to stay calm in emergencies? He's there when you handle a crisis without panicking.

Your teacher who showed you how to break down complex problems? She's there when you approach something overwhelming and know how to tackle it piece by piece.

Your cousin who taught you it's okay to take the scenic route sometimes? They're there when you slow down to enjoy something instead of rushing past it.

You don't realize how much you appreciate something until somebody takes it away.

They're not driving. But their influence is still active. Their miles are still accumulating because you're still applying what they taught you.

That's what legacy actually is. Not monuments or bank accounts or possessions divided among heirs.

It's the way someone's presence continues affecting how you drive long after they've stopped.

What You're Building Right Now

Every time you show up for someone—really show up, not just physically present but actually there—you're building your legacy.

Every time you make someone feel capable instead of inadequate, you're leaving something IN them.

Every time you show patience instead of impatience, you're teaching someone how to handle frustration.

Every time you stay present instead of distracted, you're showing someone what it means to value the moment you're in.

You're not building a monument. You're not accumulating achievements for your eulogy. You're not collecting evidence that you mattered.

You're influencing how people drive. Right now. Today. At this moment.

That's YOUR legacy.

Not what you'll leave behind when you're gone. What you're leaving IN people while you're here.

The Only Competition That Matters for This

Competing against yourself, like we talked about before, means being better today than you were yesterday.

It means asking yourself: am I making people feel more capable or less capable than yesterday? Am I showing up more present or more distracted? Am I influencing people toward patience or toward anxiety?

You're competing with yesterday's version of yourself as a presence in other people's lives.

Not those "was I more successful?" Not "did I achieve more?"

But "did I make the people around me feel more capable of handling their own routes?"

That's the competition that determines what you actually leave behind.

The Steering Wheel You Control

You control your presence. You control your example. You control whether you make someone's drive easier or harder by how you show up in their passenger seat.

You don't control their route. You don't control their destination. You don't control whether they remember you fondly or whether their memory focuses on moments you wish you could redo.

But you control who you are right now, in this moment, with the people riding with you.

And that matters.

Years from now, when you're not there anymore, they're still going to be driving with something you gave them.

What do you want that to be?

Not what you want them to think about you. Not how you want to be remembered. But what do you want to leave IN them that makes their drive better?

Your patience? Your way of thinking through problems? Your ability to stay calm when things get chaotic? Your refusal to compare their route to anyone else's?

That's what actually stays. That becomes part of how they navigate their own lives.

Legacy isn't about you. It's about them.

What you leave IN people—that's what matters. Living a life worth remembering.

That's what lasts. That continues influencing routes you'll never drive.

The car gets sold. The money gets spent. The house gets passed down or sold off.

But the way you made someone feel? The approach to life you showed? The confidence you built in them? The perspective you shared?

That stays. That becomes part of their odometer. That keeps accumulating miles long after you've stopped driving.

There is no exam grading whether you left the right amount of money or the perfect inheritance.

There's just the people you rode with, the influence you had, and what they carry forward because you were there.

That's the legacy that matters.

And you're building it right now.

Part Eight

PULLING OVER

Reaching my destination, yours still ahead.

Chapter 22

BEYOND YOUR REARVIEW

Mile by mile, your rearview mirror shows you something you can't control.

You've spent this entire drive learning about your route. Your odometer. Your steering wheel. Your pace. Everything happening on the road around you, everything you can see while you're driving.

But what about after?

What happens when someone takes an exit you're not taking? When they merge into traffic and disappear from your view? When the cars behind you become dots in the distance, then vanish entirely?

Part Eight is about what continues beyond your rearview mirror.

Those cars that were right behind you twenty minutes ago? They're dots now. Some took exits. Some changed lanes. Some are still back there somewhere, but you can't tell which ones anymore.

They're all continuing on routes you'll never see. Routes you affected without knowing where they led.

That's what this last stretch explores.

The Influence You Release

There was a movie in the '90s called *Twenty Bucks*. The entire plot follows one specific twenty-dollar bill as it passes from person to person. A wedding gift becomes a stripper's tip, then it becomes a homeless man's meal, then it becomes someone's bus fare. Each person has their moment with the bill, then it moves on to the next hand, traveling through lives and stories the previous holder will never see.

Your influence works exactly like that twenty-dollar bill.

You affect someone. Maybe you let them merge. Maybe you said good morning when they needed to hear a human voice. Maybe you held the door when they were carrying too much. That influence moves into their life, becomes part of how they see the world, and potentially affects how they treat the next person. And then it keeps traveling—hand to hand, life to life, route to route.

You never get to follow where it goes.

Imagine if you could. Imagine if you had that omniscient camera from the movie, tracking your influence like it tracked that twenty-dollar bill. You'd see exactly where your small acts traveled. Through your neighborhood. Through your city. Through people you'll never meet, who were influenced by someone you influenced, who was influenced by something you did on a Tuesday morning when you weren't even thinking about it.

For better or worse, you'd see the complete ripple. Every wave. Every direction your influence traveled. Every route it changed.

But you can't. You don't get that camera. You just release your influence into the world and trust it's traveling to places beyond your visibility.

And sometimes—more often than you'd think—that influence creates ripples you'll never see. Changes routes in ways you'll never know about. Affects people you'll never meet.

The Traffic Jam Stories

Whenever there's a traffic jam in a movie, the camera does the same thing. Wide aerial shot scanning across hundreds of cars, then zooms in to find the main character's vehicle. Everyone else is just traffic. Background. Extras. Obstacles in the protagonist's story.

What if this time, the camera zoomed OUT instead? What if we could pick any car in this traffic jam and follow its story backward?

The woman in the blue sedan. She woke up at 5:30 a.m. this morning even though she didn't need to be at work until 9 a.m. Made breakfast for her daughter. Packed a lunch. She's not from this city— she moved here three years ago for a job that promised advancement but hasn't delivered. She's thinking about her mother back home, who's getting older and might need her soon. The traffic jam is making her late for the meeting that might finally change things, or might confirm she needs to start looking elsewhere.

Go back further. Ten years. She was in college, entirely different city, dating someone she thought she'd marry until she didn't. Her parents wanted her to move back home after graduation, but she refused. That decision—that refusal—led her to this city, this job, this moment stuck in traffic thinking about whether she had made the right choices.

And we're only fantasizing about one person's backstory. One car. In a jam with hundreds of them.

That's the awareness that opens your eyes. Every person you encountered today—the security guard at the bank, the cashier at the market, the person who cut you off without signaling—they all have a backstory this deep. They were all kids once, with favorite toys and favorite cartoons and dreams about what their life would look like when they grew up.

And if everyone has a backstory that complex leading them to this exact moment, then everyone also has a forward story. Where they go after intersecting with you. What happens next on their route after your paths crossed for those few seconds.

Your influence—your slight gesture or your moment of impatience —becomes part of that forward story. We only see the parts of people that we want to see—but your influence reaches parts of them you'll never witness. Part of where they go next on routes you'll never see.

The Routes They Took After You

You let someone merge. They waved thanks. You both kept driving.

Where were they going? Maybe they were rushing to catch a flight for their grandma's funeral. Maybe your gesture—those three seconds you gave them—made the difference between making that flight and missing it. Between saying goodbye and living with regret.

Or maybe they were just going to the grocery store, and you saved them thirty seconds.

You'll never know which one.

Right now, somewhere on social media, there might be a post: "Thank you to the stranger who let me merge this morning when I was late for the most important interview of my life." You'll never see that post. You don't even know their names. You just created space, they merged, you kept driving.

That coworker who's been struggling—maybe they're dealing with a family illness, maybe they're just barely holding it together. Or the exchange student far from home trying to navigate a completely new environment. You don't have to dig into their lives. You don't need their backstory to know that reaching this moment in front of you probably took more effort than you realize.

If you meaningfully help them—if you show patience when they make a mistake, if you include them when they look lost, if you acknowledge them when everyone else treats them like furniture—you become part of their odometer starting today. Part of the route they'll remember when they think about this time in their life.

The cashier having a terrible morning until someone looked them in the eye and said good morning. The security guard who gets treated like a fixture until someone remembers they're a person. The stranger carrying too much who just needed someone to hold the door without making them feel like a burden.

Your small acts change where they go next. And then they drive away. Take exits. Merge into lanes you'll never travel. Continue on routes you'll never see.

And whatever happened next in their journey—wherever your

influence traveled in their thinking, their choices, their treatment of the next person—that's beyond your visibility now.

The Neighbor's Name

Sometimes, we're completely blind to the people close to us. Two years ago, I had a silent fight with my neighbor over a trash spot. Simple thing. Stupid thing. The spot was right at the midpoint between our properties on the sidewalk, and we'd both lived there less than a year. Almost every night, whoever took their trash out second would push the other person's bags to their side.

Petty. But it kept happening.

Then one day I snapped. Saw him doing it through the window. Stepped outside yelling. We argued. Eventually agreed to keep the trash in the same spot but facing our respective houses. Argument ended. I went back inside.

Ten minutes later I told my wife: "I'm going to his door."

She thought I was going there to pick a fight.

I rang the bell. "Hi, it's me, your neighbor."

"I'm here to apologize."

Explained I'd had a bad day at work. That I snapped. That there was no excuse for yelling at him over something as stupid as a garbage spot.

He smiled. We exchanged phone numbers.

His name is Charly.

That detail matters because until that moment, he was just "the neighbor." An obstacle. Someone making my life harder. The second I apologized, the second I admitted I was wrong, he became a person with a name. Someone I'd get to know. Someone who'd become a nicer neighbor —waving when we see each other, looking out for each other's properties.

That changed visibly between us.

How did that moment affect his life beyond our neighborly interactions? I'll never know. Besides, that wasn't my reason for doing it.

Did it change how he thinks about conflict? When someone loses their temper with him now—at work, with family, with friends—does he remember his neighbor came back ten minutes later to apologize? Does that make him more likely to de-escalate instead of holding grudges?

How did that apology ripple through his parenting? His friendships? His worldview about people who snap?

I do not know, and I don't need to. That was never the reason I went back. I wasn't trying to create any ripple effect or teach a lesson about conflict resolution. Maybe it changed nothing—maybe he was already a cool guy, and I just didn't know it yet. Maybe the apology mattered to him, maybe it didn't.

His route continued beyond my rearview mirror. I can see we're good neighbors now. Everything else? That's beyond where I can see.

The Influence That Hurts

It's not just positive ripples. Sometimes your influence creates damage you never see.

You merged without signaling. Didn't notice the car behind you had to hard stop to avoid crashing. The kid in their backseat shook, started crying. Mother got stressed and couldn't pull over on the elevated highway to comfort her child. You drove on completely unaware of this happening.

Your impatience affected someone's route, and you had no idea.

Or you're at the checkout counter. Cashier makes a mistake scanning something. You show frustration—not yelling, just a look, maybe a high sigh. They're already having a rough day. Already feeling inadequate. Your reaction confirms their fear that they're bad at their job.

They go home feeling worse about themselves because of a two-second interaction you forgot about immediately.

You said something dismissive to someone who was barely holding it together. Your comment—meant as a joke, or just thoughtless—became the thing that pushed them over into quitting the job.

You were impatient with someone doing their best. Didn't realize they were new, or dealing with something difficult, or already feeling like they couldn't do anything right.

The point isn't to make you paranoid about every interaction. The point is this: your influence spreads in directions you can't see. Sometimes positive. Sometimes negative. Usually you'll never know which.

Just like that twenty-dollar bill doesn't know whether it bought someone's medication or fed someone's addiction. It just travels from hand to hand, creating impacts beyond its awareness.

Same with your influence.

The Math Nobody Tracks

Three small acts today. Let someone merge. Say good morning. Holding a door.

Now imagine those three people each do the same—letting three people merge, greeting three strangers, holding three doors. You've gone from three to twelve people affected (3+9).

Those nine on each branch, affect three more. Now you're at thirty-nine people (3+9+27).

Watch what happens when you keep going. Thirty-nine becomes 120 (3+9+27+81). 120 becomes 363 (3+9+27+81+243). The numbers start compounding fast. By the fifth iteration, you're over a thousand people (1,093). By the seventh, you're almost at ten thousand (9,841).

Ten iterations later? 265,719 people.

Three acts. 265,719 people.

So yeah, "let's change the world one merge at a time" isn't just a nice saying for this book. The math actually supports it.

And it's completely invisible.

You're not tracking any of this while letting someone merge. You're just acting in that moment. One point or the other, we all must make that choice. And that single choice multiplies through lives you'll never meet, creating moments you'll never witness, affecting routes that branch into other routes that branch into other routes.

The influence compounds at a scale you can't measure. That's not a limitation—that's the power of it.

What This Might Change for You

Maybe this book changes how you appreciate your life and the people around you. We all would like to be the better version of ourselves. Maybe you stop living in countdown mode, stop feeling graded every day, start driving without that constant pressure of being measured against everyone else's route.

Maybe it doesn't. Maybe you expected it to be framed differently. Maybe your friend told you it was something else. Maybe you're just not in a place where any of this resonates.

Maybe you agreed with everything, but nothing changes because reading isn't the same as implementing.

Or maybe just one sentence somewhere shifted everything for you, and the rest was just context leading to that moment.

I'll never know which one.

This book is the influence I'm releasing onto your route. It's traveling with you now into places I'll never see. Maybe it changes things. Maybe it doesn't. Maybe it matters more than I could imagine, or maybe you'll forget about it entirely.

That's what happens when influence travels beyond your rearview mirror. You release it. You trust it goes where it needs to go. And you keep driving forward without knowing the outcome.

The same thing happens with every small act you create. Every gesture. Every moment where your route intersected with someone else's and your influence became part of where they went next.

You just release it and keep driving.

Beyond Your Visibility

No dashboard monitoring where your small acts traveled. No report card tracking how many people were affected by that thing you did that one morning when you were just trying to be decent.

You just drive. You create moments. You affect routes. And then those people continue on paths you'll never see, to destinations you'll never know, carrying influence you released without knowing where it would go.

Some of that influence continues for years. Decades. Maybe generations. Traveling through routes so far removed from yours that the connection back to your original act would be impossible to trace even if you could see it.

That's not a failure to track. That's not something you should've monitored better. That's just how influence works when everyone's driving their own route.

Your rearview mirror shows people for a moment after your routes intersect. Then they merge away. Take exits. Drop behind you. And their route continues beyond your visibility.

Ever wanted to be an influencer? Well, you are one. You might see yourself as ordinary. But ordinary acts create ripples you'll never see.

You influenced someone. You changed something. You created a moment that became part of where they went next.

But what happened after that? Where they went? What your influence changed in ways you can't see?

That's beyond your rearview mirror.

And you keep driving forward on your own route, creating more moments, affecting more people, releasing more influence into directions you'll never see.

There is no exam grading whether you tracked it all correctly.

There's just the route ahead, the small acts you create, and the trust that your influence is traveling to places beyond your visibility—changing routes you'll never drive, affecting people you'll never meet, creating ripples you'll never see.

That's the territory beyond your rearview mirror.

And it's bigger than you'll ever know.

Chapter 23

CRUISE CONTROL OFF

Even after thousands of miles driving the same way, you can change.

Miles back, you were measuring yourself against everyone.

Every car that passed you felt like a failure. Every car you passed felt like winning. You were competing with imaginary opponents on a highway that never had a finish line.

You were living as if there was an exam. Like someone was grading your speed, your route, your choices. Like there was a scorecard somewhere tracking whether you were driving correctly.

Now look at you.

You know you're your own reference point. You understand your route is yours—not better or worse than anyone else's, just yours. You see today as 100% of your life, not preparation for something else. You focus on your steering wheel, not everyone else's speed. You're building a legacy through presence, not through what you'll leave behind when you park.

You're not the same driver who started this journey.

What Actually Shifted

Maybe everything changed. Maybe just one thing. Maybe something in between.

But something shifted.

You stopped racing cars that were never competing with you. You stopped comparing your odometer to everyone else's mileage. You stopped thinking the lane belonged to you. You stopped honking at every perceived slight.

You started seeing other drivers as people on their own routes instead of obstacles in yours. You started measuring progress against yesterday's you instead of everyone around you. You started understanding that your memories belong to you and their memories belong to them.

You unlearned competition. You unlearned division. You unlearned the advice trap. You unlearned regret.

Not because you're done learning. Not because you figured everything out. Not because you graduated from a program or completed some course on Udemy.

But because you spent these miles examining how you drive, and somewhere along the way, your perspective changed.

The highway looks different now. Not because the highway changed. But because you're seeing it differently.

This Is Your Life Now

You didn't learn a philosophy. You didn't adopt a method. You didn't memorize a system.

You changed how you see.

And that's not something you turn on and off. That's not something you apply when convenient. That's not a technique you use in certain situations.

This is just how you drive now.

Every morning you wake up, there's no exam that day. Nobody's grading whether you're living correctly. Nobody's measuring your progress against a universal standard. Nobody's ranking you against everyone else who's also trying to figure out how to navigate their route.

Every interaction you have, there's no grade being recorded. No scorecard marking whether you handled it perfectly. No judge determining if your response was optimal.

Every choice you make, there's no universal right answer. Just the choice that makes sense for your route, at your pace, with your specific circumstances that nobody else fully understands because they're not driving your car.

This isn't philosophy anymore. This is your actual life.

You don't "practice" seeing yourself as your own reference point. You are just your own reference point. That's how perspective works.

You don't "remember" to focus on your steering wheel. You just naturally focus there now because you understand that's what you can control.

You don't "try" to see today as 100% of your life. You just see it that way now because you understand this moment is the only one you're actually living.

The shift has already happened. It's not something you're working toward. It's something you are.

The Highway Hasn't Changed

This book ends.

The traffic doesn't.

Tomorrow morning, you'll get in your car, and the highway will look exactly the same. Same lanes. Same rules. Same other drivers navigating their own routes at their own speeds.

Culture will still try to program you. Social media will still try to measure you. Society will still try to compare you. Family will still try to compete through you.

Your hometown will still judge you by your car. Your neighbors will still care about your house. Your relatives will still ask when you're getting married, having kids, or getting promoted.

The gossip cycle will still spin. The status games will still run. The imaginary competitions will still exist in everyone else's minds.

None of that changed because you read a book.

The highway operates the same way it always has. The other cars are still driving like there's an exam. The culture is still broadcasting the same message. The programming is still running on every screen, in every conversation, through every interaction.

But you're different.

You see it differently now. You respond to it differently now. You drive through it differently now. Without the constant stress. Without the weight of imaginary grades. Without anxiety about how you measure up.

The stress you used to carry—constantly being measured, constantly comparing, constantly feeling graded—that weight lifted somewhere along this journey. Not because the world stopped being stressful. But because you stopped believing the stress was necessary.

You're not competing, so you can't lose. You're not being graded, so you can't fail. You're not racing, so you can't fall behind.

The pressure is still there. But it doesn't land on you the same way anymore. Perhaps we are asking the wrong questions—not "Am I winning?" but "Am I driving?"

When culture tells you to compete, you recognize the infinite loop before you enter it. When social media tries to grade you, you remember nobody's actually keeping score. When society measures you against arbitrary standards, you know you're measuring against yesterday's you instead.

The pressure didn't disappear. You just stopped believing it.

The comparisons didn't stop. You just stopped taking part.

The imaginary exam didn't vanish. You just realized it was never real.

And that's enough.

You don't need the world to change. You don't need everyone else to stop competing. You don't need culture to stop programming or social media to stop measuring or society to stop comparing.

You just need to keep driving your route at your pace with your focus on your own steering wheel.

The highway is the same. You're different.

That's what matters.

Conscious Driving

For how many miles were you on cruise control?

Following the speed everyone around you was going. Staying in the lane culture told you to drive. Taking the exit society expected. Competing because that's what you learned to do. Measuring because that's what you were taught mattered. You know that feeling—not sure if you're awake or asleep?

Autopilot. Programmed responses. Automatic reactions. Cultural scripts running without your conscious involvement.

You weren't really driving. You were being driven—by expectations, by programming, by inherited beliefs about what success means and how life should look and what you're supposed to want.

But you've been driving manually for miles now—maybe you just noticed.

You took manual control. Free your mind from the cruise control settings someone else programmed. You started making conscious choices instead of automatic ones. You started questioning whether the route everyone else takes is the route that makes sense for you.

You're driving now. Actually driving.

Not perfectly. Not without mistakes. Not without occasionally forgetting and slipping back into old patterns.

But consciously. Intentionally. With the awareness that you're the one holding the wheel, pressing the pedals, choosing the lanes, deciding the speed.

Cruise control is off. And you're not turning it back on.

What You Carry Forward

This awareness doesn't leave.

It's not something you'll forget when you close this book. It's not something that wears off when you get back to your regular life. It's not temporary clarity that fades when the real world rushes back in.

You can't unsee what you've seen. You can't unknow what you now understand. Understanding it isn't the same as living it.

You'll be reminded every single day. Every time you get in your actual car, start your engine, pull onto your actual commute—you'll remember. The highway isn't just a place you're reading about. It's where you live.

You'll still face pressure. You'll still encounter competition. You'll still hear voices telling you to measure yourself against everyone else.

But you'll recognize it now. You'll see it for what it is. And you'll choose whether to engage or keep your eyes on your own road.

Some days you'll drive with perfect clarity, remembering everything you've learned, navigating with confidence.

Some days you'll slip back into old patterns, start comparing yourself to others, feel the pull of imaginary competitions.

Both are fine. Both are part of driving your route. You're not trying to achieve perfect consistency. You're just trying to drive more consciously more often than you did before.

And you will. Once you see there's no exam, you can't pretend it exists. Once you understand you're your own reference point, you can't measure yourself from someone else's coordinates. Once you recognize your route is yours, you can't drive like you're on someone else's path.

The shift is permanent. Not because you'll never forget. But even when you forget, you'll remember again. The awareness is there now. It doesn't disappear just because you're not thinking about it every moment.

You're Ready

For this entire drive, we've been traveling together.

I've been pointing things out. Showing you what I've noticed. Sharing a perspective that helped me stop living like there was an exam grading my every move.

You've been processing it. Testing it against your own experience. Deciding what resonates and what doesn't. Making it yours instead of just accepting it. This was for you, and you alone.

And now you're ready.

Not because you've mastered everything. Not because you've figured it all out. Not because you'll never struggle with these concepts again.

But because you understand them now. The perspective has shifted. The awareness exists. The cruise control is off. You already know what you have to do.

You're ready to keep driving—consciously, intentionally, with your eyes on your own road instead of everyone else's.

The highway hasn't changed. The traffic is still there. The pressure still exists.

But you're different. And that's what matters.

You're not the driver you were when we started this drive. You're not measuring yourself against imaginary standards anymore. You're not competing in races that don't exist. You're not living as if there's an exam.

You're just driving. Your route. Your pace. Your choices. We are still here. You're still on the road. That's what matters.

And that's exactly what you're supposed to be doing.

Because there is no exam. There never was.

There's just you on your route, driving toward whatever comes next.

Cruise control is off.

You're ready.

Chapter 24

THIS IS MY STOP

S o the moment has come. We arrived together at this point and this is where I get off.

Not because the journey ends. Your route continues. But this particular ride we've been on together—this conversation we've been having for the last few hundred miles—this is where it naturally concludes.

What This Actually Was

I wasn't teaching you how to live. I don't have your answers. I can't. You're driving a route I've never driven, navigating conditions I've never faced, making choices based on circumstances I don't fully understand because they're yours, not mine.

What I did was share perspective. I pointed out patterns I noticed on my route. I showed you what helped me stop living like there was an exam grading every choice I make. What helped me live with less stress, less anxiety, less weight on my shoulders. A happier life.

And you processed it. You took what I shared and ran it through your own experiences, your own lens, your own understanding of how your life actually works. You decided what resonated and what didn't.

You made it yours—not by copying my route, but by using my observations to understand your own.

Remember the advice trap? That wasn't just about other people's advice. That was also the entire book. If you try to drive the route exactly as I described it, you'll crash. Because my route isn't your route. My obstacles aren't your obstacles. My destination isn't your destination.

This was a conversation between two people on different routes who happened to be traveling in the same direction for a while. I shared what I saw. You decided what it meant to you.

That's all this was. And that's exactly what it needed to be.

You See Differently Now

You can spot programming everywhere now. You can't unsee it.

Take celebrity beauty, for example. We praise famous people for being gorgeous, but if that same person wasn't famous, if they weren't wealthy, if they were just working at the corner store, we might not even notice them. Their *doppelgänger* exists somewhere, with the exact same face, the exact same body, the exact same features. But we don't fantasize about the replica. We don't put the unknown twin on magazine covers.

We're not actually praising beauty. We're praising position. We're worshipping status and calling it aesthetics. But is it truth? Or just an illusion?

Same with your boss's jokes. People laugh harder because of the role, not because the humor improved.

The same bands get pushed with massive marketing budgets and become global sensations, while musicians with more talent, better choreography, and superior skill remain unknown.

We praise the famous ones not because they're better, but because we're programmed to worship what's already been elevated.

You see that now. It's obvious. You're more aware of the pattern.

Or look at how we build technology. Every new humanoid robot gets announced with the same fanfare—"Look, it can do household chores!"

But why are we fixated on copying the human body? If the goal is usefulness, why stick to two arms instead of four? I mean, hello there... (yes, that's a *Star Wars* reference).

We're not building robots to help us. We're building them to look like us. We're racing ourselves as a species. Trying to beat the human form instead of solving actual problems.

The car became autonomous without needing a robot to sit in the driver's seat. The laundry system could be THE robot instead of building a person-shaped machine to operate the washer.

But we keep competing with our own body design like there's an exam somewhere grading whether we successfully replicated ourselves.

Even the phrase "think outside the box" it's programming. The box is the programming.

Don't think outside the box. Think like there's no box.

Don't let the programming be your reference point. Always question whether the box exists at all.

But the most important shift? The one that changes your actual daily life?

You don't see NPCs anymore.

You used to see the barista as someone who should make your coffee faster. The driver going slow as an obstacle in your way. The cashier who made a mistake as someone who should be better at their job. Functions that should perform efficiently.

Now you see opportunities.

Every interaction is a chance to recognize another human. To see the person behind the function. To practice showing up as human instead of treating people like background scenery in your story.

You went from entitled to service to grateful for the opportunity. From frustrated by obstacles to appreciating each moment where you can see someone fully instead of reducing them to their role.

The barista isn't there to serve you. They're people who are making coffee today, just like you're a person who is ordering it. That's an opportunity to connect, even briefly, as two humans sharing space instead of one person extracting service from another.

That's *omoiyari* living in you now. Not as something you practice. As something you see.

There's another layer to this.

You don't see divisions anymore.

Your hometown taught you there's us and them. Your group and other groups. Your people and those people. Teams. Tribes. Categories. Hierarchies.

You see through that now.

Everyone's just a driver on their own route. No teams. No hierarchy. No more us versus them. Just individuals navigating their own highways at their own pace with their own destinations that have nothing to do with yours.

The programming tried to make you think in divisions. You don't anymore.

You can't unsee any of this now. Seeing is believing. The vision shift is permanent. Not because you're trying to maintain it, but because once you see clearly, you can't pretend the blur was real.

The Real Challenge

We just acknowledged you're ready. That you've changed. That cruise control is off.

All of that's true.

But here's the harder part: staying this way.

The world hasn't changed. Culture still programs. Social media still measures. Society still compares. Everyone around you still drives like there's an exam.

And the pull back is constant.

You'll be in line at the supermarket and feel that old frustration rising—why is this person so slow, don't they know I have places to be —before you catch yourself and remember: they're not an NPC. They're a person having a day just as real as yours.

You'll see someone's success on social media and feel that comparison creeping in—they're ahead, you're behind, you're not doing enough—before you remember: your odometer measures your miles, not theirs.

You'll hear your hometown's voice in your head—you should want this, you should value that, you should compete here—before you remember: those are inherited beliefs, not your authentic desires.

The programming doesn't stop running just because you can see it now.

This isn't about daily affirmations or mantras. This isn't about reminding yourself every morning that there's no exam. This is about driving intentionally in a world designed to put you back on autopilot.

Can you keep seeing the humans when everyone treats them as functions? Can you keep your eyes on your road when everyone's watching everyone else's speed? Can you keep driving your route when culture keeps telling you which route you should take instead?

You can. Not perfectly. Not every moment. Not without occasionally slipping back into old patterns.

But more often than before. And when you slip, you'll notice faster. You'll catch yourself sooner. You'll return to conscious driving more quickly.

Because the awareness is there now. It doesn't leave. It's not something you're working to maintain. It's just part of how you see.

What You're Driving With

Complete others rather than compete with them. The L in "complete" gets you the W.

In your team. In your family. In your relationship. In your work. Completing others means everyone wins. Competing means someone has to lose. You don't need to race everyone. Not everything is a competition. There's no exam.

Control what you can control. Your steering wheel. Your speed. Your lane. Your choices. That's it. You can't control the traffic. You can't control the weather. You can't control what other drivers do. Focus on what's actually in your hands. Everything else is just noise.

Your memories belong to you. Nobody else was in your head when you lived those moments. They can't change what you experienced. They can't tell you what it meant. Your memories are yours alone—not up for debate, not subject to someone else's interpretation. What you lived is what you lived.

You see others as human. Not as NPCs. Not as obstacles. Not as functions. People with full lives that are just as real and complex as yours. Every interaction is an opportunity to recognize that. To show up as human instead of just extracting what you need and moving on.

Today is 100% of your life. Not a fraction waiting for completion. Not preparation for tomorrow. This is it. The life you're living right now is the only one you're actually experiencing.

Go and tell someone what they mean to you.

Today.

Say the important thing you've been waiting for the "right moment" to say. You're not in countdown mode—there's no timer running out. But today is 100% of what you have, so live it like it matters. Because it does.

Not everyone will reach the same distance as you. Some routes end before others. That's not a failure. That's not falling behind. That's just life. Some people's journeys conclude earlier than expected. Some later. You don't know which one is gonna be yours.

That's not meant to scare you. It's meant to make today matter even more. Not in a countdown way. But in the present, intentional way. You're here now. The people you can reach today are here now. Call them.

My Exit

You're continuing on your route. Our paths diverge now.

That's not abandonment. That's just how routes work. We traveled together for these miles. We had this conversation. We shared this stretch of highway.

But your route continues beyond where mine stops. And that's exactly how it should be.

You've got the wheel. You've always had it, actually. Look closely. The driver was always you. Your hands. Your choices. Your direction. I was never driving for you. I couldn't. It's your car. Your route. Your life.

All I did was ride along and point out what I noticed. Share observations. Offer perspective. But every mile you traveled? That was you driving. Every shift in how you see things? That was you changing. Every choice about what resonated? That was you deciding.

You don't need me to point things out anymore. You can see them yourself now.

The programming is visible to you. The NPCs have become human. The divisions have dissolved. The imaginary exam has been revealed for what it always was—nothing. There's no magic here—just the realization that was there all along.

You see your route for what it is: yours.

You've been holding the map this whole time. Your atlas. Your route.

Not better or worse than anyone else's. Not ahead or behind. Not winning or losing. Just yours.

And that's enough.

There is no exam. There never was. Nobody's grading your route. Nobody's ranking your choices. Nobody's keeping score of whether you're doing life correctly.

There's just you on your route, driving toward whatever comes next.

You know where your reference point is, and you may have passed several "obstacles" to get here. But now you are seeing some drivers on the road. And you are going to get to them, so that you can achieve the success you need. You've already realized who you are competing against. You already know what your 100% means. You know which choices brought you to this moment. You are here. You know not everyone will reach the same distance as you. Previous generations told you how to drive, but now you know your eyes just need to be focused on the road ahead. No distractions. You know all of this. You always have.

Ready? Take the wheel.

APPENDIX A: CHECK ENGINE

On November 25, 2022, I got diagnosed with Asperger's. I was 45 years old.

Asperger's is now merged into the autism spectrum, since the latest DSM. I'm autistic (and very proud!). The diagnosis changed my life—not because it changed who I am, but because it finally explained why I process the world the way I do.

I went through the three-step inclusion journey I described in the book: Awareness > Acceptance > Indifference. That last one is positive. Like being left-handed. Different wiring. Not deficient. Just different.

The diagnosis gave me two things. First, explanations for patterns I'd lived with my entire life. I'm hypersensitive to noise, so now I avoid loud places instead of forcing myself to endure them without knowing I was masking. I always needed things to make literal sense. I couldn't accept vague social rules without questioning them. Now I know why.

Second, it helped me embrace a perspective I've always had—this need to see things from different angles, to question what everyone else accepts as normal.

That's where the content of this book came from. My Asperger's brain needs literal answers. When I see competition everywhere, my brain immediately thinks: ok, so what's the prize? When does it end? What are the rules?

And when I couldn't find answers to those questions—when I realized there IS no prize, there IS no end, there ARE no rules—my brain concluded: then there's no competition.

That realization became "There Is No Exam." Once I saw that pattern in competition, I started seeing it everywhere. All these invisible grading systems people stress about—none of them actually exist. They're abstract social constructs we've all agreed to treat as real.

And because of my autism, I can't accept abstract social constructs without evidence. If someone tells me, "You need to keep up with others," my brain immediately asks: "Keep up with which others? By what metric? Who's measuring? Who decided this?"

It may look like I'm defying authority, but I'm genuinely looking for answers. Or when someone says goodbye like "take care!" I'm like: "Well, obviously I'll take care of myself."

So, my initial take was about writing a book about the POV of an autistic person in life, but then I decided to avoid that route because first, if I mentioned my autism upfront I knew it might predispose people to think the book was about autism—I can read the room (pun intended)—and that's why I didn't make the tagline "An Autistic Approach To Life" or anything like that. And second, this is me embracing the Indifference phase, meaning that I don't need to announce my diagnosis. This book is for everyone. And the message works whether or not you knew I'm autistic.

My Backstory

I'm not a psychologist. I'm not a therapist. I have no formal training in human behavior or mental health.

I studied mechanical engineering. I worked 13+ years in sports. Publishing. Evolved into tech. Being around the 'Silicon Valley' type of companies five years now. I've spent my career as an AI Product Manager in R&D, building digital products and solving problems. That's my background. Analytical. Technical. Empirical.

I even created a webpage about me treated as software versioning:

https://ericsalinas.dev I share tech-related thoughts in there, but the core experiment was for me to share my development as versioning with patches, minor and major upgrades. I also share my book updates, so if you ever visit, don't forget to look under the hood. That's me in a nutshell. I'm weird and I love it.

This book didn't come from academic credentials. It's coming from my route—the specific experiences and circumstances that gave me this perspective.

(Yes, it's coming from my heart, but my fixation on staying in metaphor won this internal battle.)

APPENDIX B: WHEN THEY RUN OUT OF GAS

Back in 2022, during our Neurodiversity Talks at Wizeline (where I currently work), one day the topic turned to fearing the death of our loved ones—specifically our parents. I shared my perspective on death, and people told me it helped them think about loss differently. I'm sharing it here just in case it may help someone:

Because of my autism and Asperger's, I'm very pragmatic about death.

I don't fear it. Not because I'm brave or enlightened or detached. But because death is a fact. It can't be undone. It's inevitable.

Even now, with all the advances in GenAI, you can't recreate a loved one. You could train an LLM on their voice, their behavior patterns, their writing style. You could create a realistic avatar that looks like them. You could generate responses that sound like something they'd say.

But they'd still be gone. The person who actually existed, who actually lived, who actually influenced your life—that person is gone. Technology doesn't change that.

That's why I don't fear death.

What I Actually Worry About

I do worry when someone dies. But not about the person who died.

I worry about the people left behind. The ones who are suffering because of the loss. The ones trying to figure out how to keep living without someone who was part of their daily existence.

Other people. Not me.

Everyone mourns and handles loss differently, and that's okay—and expected. I'm not saying it's not okay to mourn. I'm not saying grief is wrong or that people should "get over it" quickly.

But here's where my autism shows up: when someone dies, they can't suffer anymore. They're gone. The suffering stays with the people who are still here, still alive, still having to navigate life without them.

Celebrating Lives, Not Just Mourning Deaths

When Bob Barker (the host from The *Price is Right*) died, I saw a tweet that said, "We lost Bob at 99 years old. What a sad thing!"

And I thought: sad? He lived for 99 years!

I'm not saying people can't be sad. Grief is real. Loss hurts.

But 99 years. That's almost a full century of life. That's decades of influence, achievement, relationships, experiences. That's setting standards for game show television that lasted generations.

That's a life fully lived.

We should celebrate this milestone. Celebrate his life and achievements. Not just mourn that he's gone.

On the other side of that, tragic deaths—young people, unexpected losses, lives cut short—those are always sad. Nobody deserves to die young.

But even then, we always have the chance to celebrate their lives. The impact they created when they were here. The lessons they left behind. The influence they had on people around them, on society, on their loved ones.

We're all going to die. And using Paul Heyman's phrase: "That's not a prediction, that's a spoiler".

Most times, your parents are going to die before you. And no parent would want to experience the opposite if asked. Believe me, I've experienced that opposite.

You may or may not be prepared for when that happens. But you can always be ready to celebrate their lives.

Remember everything they taught you. Every moment they shared with you. All the memories you created with them. They will always be your parents, and they will always be irreplaceable.

Honor them by being the person they worked hard most of their lives for you to become the person you are right now.

"Simple" as that.

Keeping Their Spirit Alive

If you're religious, you can talk to them in prayer.

If you're not, you can replicate their behavior in your everyday life to keep their spirit alive.

You can adopt the habits they taught you. Use the wisdom they shared. Make decisions the way they showed you how. Handle challenges with the approach they showed when you watched them navigate similar situations.

That's how you honor them. Not through monuments or perfect remembrances. Through living in a way that reflects what they taught you. Through carrying forward the influence they had on who you became.

They're gone. But what they taught you—that's still here. And you get to decide whether to use it or ignore it.

We're afraid of them passing away tomorrow, but we're not afraid of doing nothing today. We know people won't be here forever, but we act like there's always more time.

DON'T WAIT until they die to tell them you LOVE them.

Tell them now while they're still alive. While they can still hear you say it.

Don't save appreciation for funerals. Don't hold back love until it's too late. Don't wait for the "right moment" to express what someone means to you.

The moment is always right. Say it now.

Too many people save their most honest words for eulogies. They spent the funeral talking about what that person meant to them, wishing they'd said it while the person was still alive to hear it.

Don't be that person.

Your parents are still alive? Tell them you appreciate what they taught you. Your friend is still here? Let them know their presence in your life mattered. Your partner is beside you? Make sure they understand what they mean to you.

Is it hard to share your feelings? Sorry but you don't get to play that card in front of me. I'm the autistic one here.

Say it now. Not later. Not eventually. Not when you feel ready.

Now.

Death is inevitable. Today is everyone's 100%. And once someone is gone, you can't tell them anymore. You can only wish you had.

APPENDIX C: CLEANING MY TRUNK

I'm not writing this appendix to tell you how to think. I'm writing this to show you I've had to unlearn programming too.

The bias virus I talked about in the book? I caught it. Multiple strains. And I'm still working on clearing some of it out.

When Pain Became Judgment

I struggled with sperm count and motility.

That struggle created something in me I didn't recognize at first: a strong anti-abortion bias.

I became egotistically judgmental. How could anyone choose not to have a child when we were desperately trying and couldn't? How could someone end a pregnancy when we would have done anything to be pregnant?

My pain created my judgment. I was measuring everyone else's situation against mine.

That took me to Gestalt therapy. And something shifted.

I started seeing that my reality wasn't universal. A wanted pregnancy and an unwanted pregnancy are completely distinct realities. A couple trying for years to conceive is in a different situation than a teenager who got pregnant from rape. A planned child in a stable relationship differs from an abusive situation where a woman has no control over her own body.

I'm still personally pro-life. That hasn't changed. But I've learned to respect other people's choices about their own bodies.

I mean, my male body autonomy has never been questioned. No politician has ever suggested regulating masturbation on males. Nobody ever told me what I could or couldn't do with my sperm. (Those are alive too.)

Legislation only seems to apply to women's bodies.

That double standard made me examine my position. Not abandon it. Just examine it.

That's where I landed. Not agreeing with every abortion decision. Not saying my pro-life stance was wrong. Just respecting that other people's realities differ from mine, and they get to make their own choices.

Refusing the Monterrey Script

I know this will backfire terribly if I ever run for Mayor, but there's a deep strain of *machismo* in my hometown. I'm not saying it's unique to that place—it's just the one I can speak about firsthand because I lived it.

At parties, the script was always the same: women in the kitchen, men at the grill or watching "the game". Gender-segregated spaces. Gender-divided WhatsApp groups where men shared porn. Homophobic attitudes treated as "normal."

Everyone participated. Everyone enforced it. Everyone acted as if this was just how things worked.

I refused to take part.

I sat with my wife instead of "with the guys." I left the men's WhatsApp groups when added. I didn't play along with the homophobic jokes.

And I lost friendships over it.

People didn't understand why I wasn't following the script. Why I wasn't taking part in the culture everyone else accepted as normal. Why I was choosing to sit with the women instead of where I was "supposed" to be.

For me, it was simple. I wanted to sit with my wife. I refused to segregate by gender. I didn't take part in the culture I disagreed with.

But that "simple" choice came with social consequences. Some friendships faded away. I became the outsider because I wouldn't enforce the gender scripts everyone else was following.

I don't regret it (what's regret?). But I won't pretend it was easy or that it didn't cost me anything.

Refusing to take part was just the surface level though. There was a deeper unlearning I had to work through.

(The following is aimed at men.)

I noticed something in how people justified supporting feminist causes. The phrase that kept appearing was: "I support this because I have a sister/mother/wife/daughter."

Dude, that justification is still egocentric. You're only supporting the cause because it affects someone connected to you. You're defending women's rights because the harm to the women bounces back and affects you as a man. You're implying that if you didn't have that female relative, you wouldn't care?

That's not support. That's protecting your own territory.

Genuine support means recognizing people as people, not as extensions of your own life. Not as NPCs who only matter because they're in your storyline. It means supporting causes because other humans are being harmed—not only because those humans happen to be related to you.

I had to unlearn that egoistic framing. Stop justifying support through personal connections. Start recognizing that people's struggles matter regardless of whether they affect me or anyone I know.

What I'm Still Working On

I'm not presenting myself as someone who's cleared all bias programming. I haven't.

I still catch myself making assumptions. I still notice programming surfacing that I thought I'd unlearned. I still have moments where I realize I'm measuring someone else's situation against my reference point instead of seeing their reality.

This isn't a story about how I figured it all out. This is a story about recognizing that I absorbed programming I didn't choose, and I'm actively working to examine it.

Some of it I've cleared. Some of it I'm still processing. Some of it I probably haven't even identified yet.

The difference between now and before? I'm now aware it exists. I'm examining my automatic reactions. I'm questioning the programming instead of just following it.

That's not mastery. That's just practice.

And I'm sharing this not because I have all the answers, but because maybe seeing someone else examine their own programming makes it easier for you to examine yours.

We all caught the bias virus. Multiple strains. From multiple sources. Absorbed over years of exposure.

You don't have to keep running that programming just because it was installed in you. You can examine it. Question it. Decide whether you want to keep it or clear it out.

That's not easy. It costs something. It means recognizing that ideas you held as truth might have been programming. It means losing relationships with people who expect you to enforce the same biases they're following.

Even with family members. As my wife rightly says, "Even the family tree can be pruned."

But the alternative is living your entire life running software someone else installed in you without your permission.

I'd rather examine the code.

NOTES

3. THE ROUTES THEY TAUGHT YOU

1. Neil deGrasse Tyson, *Starry Messenger: Cosmic Perspectives on Civilization* (Henry Holt and Company, 2022), 149.
2. Neil deGrasse Tyson, *Starry Messenger*, 150.

19. RACING YOUR OWN ODOMETER

1. John C. Maxwell, *Leadershift: The 11 Essential Changes Every Leader Must Embrace* (HarperCollins Leadership, 2019), 46.
2. Mo Gawdat, *Solve for Happy: Engineer Your Path to Joy* (Gallery Books, 2017), 18.

ABOUT THE AUTHOR

Eric Salinas isn't a psychologist, therapist, or self-help guru. He's an engineer-turned-tech-professional who spent years competing in a race that didn't exist—until he realized the grading system causing his stress was something he could unlearn. This book is his conversation with anyone still feeling measured by invisible standards. He lives in Mexico with his wife Silvana, their son, and their two Shih Tzus, Wookie & Padme.

#thereisnoexam

g goodreads.com/ericsalinas

a amazon.com/author/ericsalinas

BB bookbub.com/authors/eric-salinas

in linkedin.com/in/esalinas

o instagram.com/ericsalinas21

@ threads.com/@ericsalinas21

f facebook.com/ericsalinas21

X x.com/ericsalinas

d tiktok.com/ericsalinaspie

▶ youtube.com/@ericsalinas_dev

AUTHOR'S NOTE

This book wasn't written thinking in terms of revenue or profit. This was genuinely written to spread this message.

This is the "There is No Exam" mindset trying to transcend—even after I'm gone—leaving its influence to change the world. Because let's be honest, when you think you have an amazing thought or even an amazing mind, it doesn't matter if you keep that to yourself. If it's not shared, that means it doesn't add value. Therefore, there is no point in keeping wisdom to ourselves.

So please, if you bought this book physically, share it with another person. It won't make a difference standing right there on your bookshelf as decoration. Let's help spread the influence, and to make it more traceable, before you share it, grab a pen or pencil and add your full name below, so whenever another hand gets ahold of this, they can trace the "influence" back by noticing its previous owners. And that would be the representation of the 'tree branch' for this specific book, with you being the current endpoint. You are the current: "You Are Here!"

— Eric Salinas

Previous Owners:

ACKNOWLEDGMENTS

This book exists because of Silvana.

She's a bestselling author who inspired me to write, coached me along the way, and copy edited this book. She believed I had something worth sharing with the world and supported me in writing it as my true self.

To Norma Sánchez, my therapist for over a decade: this book is essentially ten years of our sessions, distilled. There's Gestalt in every chapter, whether readers recognize it or not. Thank you for demanding I finish it—yes, *demanding*—when I needed that push.

To Jorge Matus, the guinea pig. For almost two years, you trusted me as your mentor, and that responsibility forced me to articulate things I'd only felt. Most of these shifts were crafted in our conversations, for you, because you needed to hear them. Turns out, so did I.

To Daniel Niquet, one conversation on that terrace about how we don't create others' memories became a cornerstone of this book. Some insights arrive in boardrooms; others arrive when someone is brave enough to be vulnerable with a coworker.

To Clay Griffith, who told me "you are not one in many, you're one in one" when I needed it the most. That line belongs in this book. It probably is this book.

To Willie González, who twenty years ago was curious enough to ask how I felt about making cartoons after graduating from the most expensive college in town. That question, asked the way only a friend can—with intrigue, not judgment—sparked something: my "How far can I go?" started right there.

To Victoria Cornejo, who gave me the stage. You scheduled the first "There Is No Exam" talk at Wizeline, believed in the message before it was a manuscript, and encouraged me to keep going. Mental health advocacy needs more people like you.

To Gema del Río, my dear *comadrita*, thank you for putting a spotlight on me not as a guest, but as someone whose perspective mattered. You gave me the chance to inspire your audience—my community—to embrace autism as something to carry with pride.

To Santiago Sillis, for always rooting for me and making me believe that this message matters. Sometimes that's exactly what a person needs to hear.

To my parents, Humberto and Margarita, and my sister Myriam, thank you for being there through this entire journey, supporting me in ways both visible and quiet.

To my son David, who teaches me every day that having fun and enjoying life doesn't mean doing it the way society says kids are supposed to. You've never needed permission to be yourself, and I will always be there to watch and support how far you can go.

And to you, reading this last paragraph is proof that you squeezed every last mile out of your tank to get here, and that means the world to me. I'm part of your drive now. Thank you for letting me ride along.

www.ingramcontent.com/pod-product-compliance
Lightning Source LLC
Chambersburg PA
CBHW071719120626
46550CB00001B/297